30+ Games to Get Ready to Read

ALSO BY TONI S. GOULD

*Get Ready to Read: A Practical Guide for Teaching Young Children
at Home and in School*

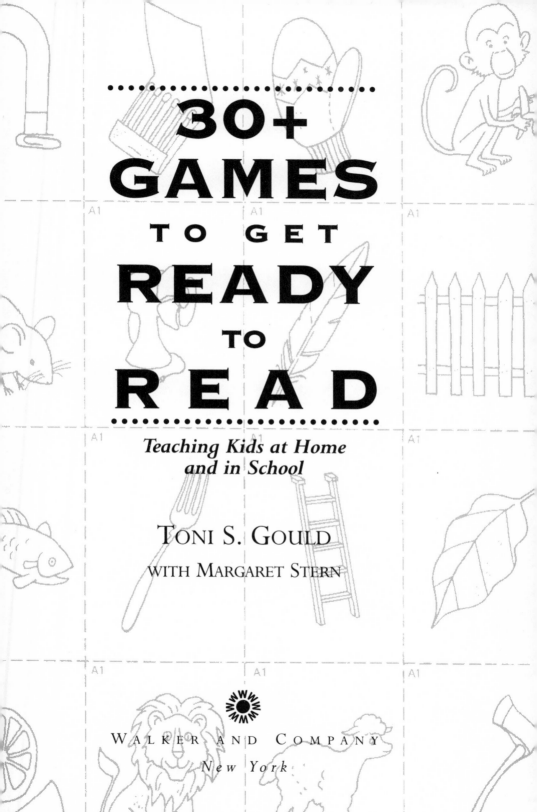

30+
GAMES
TO GET
READY
TO
READ

Teaching Kids at Home
and in School

TONI S. GOULD

WITH MARGARET STERN

WALKER AND COMPANY

New York

First published in the United States of America in 1994 by Walker Publishing Company, Inc.

Published simultaneously in Canada by Thomas Allen & Son Canada, Limited, Markham, Ontario

Library of Congress Cataloging-in-Publication Data
Gould, Toni S.
30-[plus] games to get ready to read : teaching kids at home and
in school / Toni S. Gould with Margaret Stern.
p.   cm.
On galley t.p. "[plus]" appears as a plus sign.
ISBN 0-8027-7432-6
1. Reading (Preschool)   2. Reading games.   3. Reading readiness.
I. Stern, Margaret B.   II. Title.   III. Title: Thirty-[plus] games to
get ready to read.
LB1140.R4A15   1994
372.4—dc20   94-9574
CIP

Book design by Glen M. Edelstein

Printed in the United States of America

2   4   6   8   10   9   7   5   3   1

CONTENTS

30+ Games to Get Ready to Read

INTRODUCTION

THE GAMES in this book, like other children's games, are to be played for fun. But these games are not *just* for fun; they are carefully prepared to teach children basic readiness and reading skills. While children play, they learn to read, write, and spell.

Basic to this book is the philosophy that children learn best by understanding, not by memorizing. When children learn by understanding, there is a great deal of transfer to new tasks. Transfer means children can discover a new letter or word on their own because they can apply their learning to related tasks. This kind of learning heightens their motivation and raises their self-esteem. Learning through understanding has the added advantage of challenging children's intelligence. Children become aware that they are learning through actively using their minds. Thus, playing these games furthers children's intellectual growth.

The best motivation for learning is the joy of learning. Any kind of meaningless drill on letters or words diminishes this joy significantly. If, on the other hand, children are helped to understand every step in the learning process, they can't wait to learn more. Their joy is heightened by being able to learn through playing games.

READING READINESS

READING READINESS does not spring forth spontaneously within a child at age six or six and a half. Reading readiness consists of many clearly identifiable skills. A mastery of spoken language, such as learning to speak in complete sentences, is essential before learning how to read a written sentence. A sense of direction, that is, moving from left to right (we read from left to right), auditory and visual perception, and eye-hand and fine motor coordination must be developed before children are ready to learn to read. Most important, children must be helped to develop an understanding of the sound-symbol relationship for each letter.

There is no question that a child needs sufficiently developed intellectual ability to get meaning from the printed symbol or word and that the child's nervous system must be mature enough to handle the relationship of spoken to written language. However, even if you do not see all the evidence of such maturity that you might like, at or around the age of four I strongly recommend playing readiness games with children, especially to help them develop an understanding of sound-symbol relationships. Why? Just observe typical four-year-olds. Usually they are at the height of their curiosity. "What do the squiggles [i.e., letters and words] say?" Frequently they ask, "Is that my name? Is it Mommy's name? Or Daddy's?" Their questions clearly indicate their interest in written language. Children often know when they are ready to learn to read—a time that does not necessarily coincide with the school's timetable.

Some parents or teachers may worry that an early start in teaching children readiness skills may "push" their children. A clear-cut answer to the dilemma of whether to teach or not to teach is given by Jeanne S. Chall, one of the foremost reading authorities in this country. She writes, "Doesn't an *early* knowledge of, or interest in, letters mark a new step in the child's intellectual development? Pointing to and naming a letter, or writing a letter, is quite different from pointing to or drawing a picture of a cat, a truck, or a tree."* From this vantage point, helping four-year-old children to learn sound-symbol relationships or eventually learn to read is fostering, not pushing, their intellectual development.

There is yet another advantage to teaching four-year-old children. Preschool children do not distinguish as yet between learning and playing. At four, children have time to learn and can enjoy learning through games. Clearly, the play aspect is in the foreground. That they are learning seems relatively unimportant. Not until the heavy door falls behind them do children find out that there is a difference between playing and learning and that learning is dull.

Finally, when children start learning at age four, you gain time. Some children go through the readiness stage very quickly. They arrive breathlessly at their desired goal: reading. Other children, however, progress very slowly and need lots of practice. Some children need four weeks to learn one letter. These children need more time to learn each sound-symbol relationship than the typical school kindergarten or first grade provides.

WHICH CHILDREN BENEFIT FROM THESE GAMES?

In general, we have found four categories of children who enjoy and benefit from these games:

*Jeanne S. Chall, *Learning To Read: The Great Debate* (New York: McGraw-Hill, 1967, p. 159.) Italics are mine.

1. Preschool and kindergarten children who have shown that they are eager to learn to read and write. These children really want an overall key to reading and writing, not just random pieces of information. We have found that they thrive on these games, which give them a logical and generally valid system for transposing sounds into letters and letters into sounds.

2. Preschool children whose early development has shown them to be slow developers. These children need an early start in order not to fail in school. This group includes children who began to talk relatively late, those who have a somewhat short attention span, and those with a poor auditory or visual memory. This group also includes children whose fine motor skills need developing, because they find it difficult to guide a pencil. Children for whom pediatricians or neurologists foresee difficulties or failure in school because of slow learning patterns will also benefit from an early start.

Given the opportunity and tools, it is obviously better to prevent a child's failure than to have to remedy it. In the thirty-five years since I first began using these games with these types of children as well as with children who have more severe learning difficulties, none have subsequently failed in first grade.

3. Students who have gone through first or second (or even third or fourth) grade without learning to read. With such students, I have found that reading games are far more effective than textbooks or workbooks. These students usually freeze at the sight of a book, for the simple reason that they have come to associate books with failure. This learning block is bypassed completely in the game situation. The children focus all their attention on the games and, in time, they discover—to their amazement—that they actually have begun to read. The logical sequence and the phonetically regular vocabulary (i.e., words in which each letter represents a specific sound previously learned) presented in the games give children a secure foundation in reading. Older children who have not profited from reading instruction in school can and do learn basics of reading and spelling through playing these games.

4. Bilingual students for whom English is a second language. With this group, too, the readiness and reading games have proved successful, because they introduce the student to reading in English with regular words and without any pressure to perform.

WHAT KINDS OF GAMES ARE PRESENTED HERE?

This book presents two distinct types of games: 17 readiness games and 20 reading games. The readiness games develop systematically every readiness skill essential for learning to read. The reading games help children to learn to read, write, and spell approximately 150 phonetically regular words—where each letter always has the same sound.

Children can learn the skill of reading only *after* they have developed the reading readiness skills previously mentioned. Without this foundation, most attempts to teach reading will fail.

Through pictures, children learn the meaning of new words, thus enriching their speaking vocabulary. Also, they acquire a feeling for the movement from left to right and from top to bottom. While playing, children learn how to hold and use a pencil.

THE ROLE OF THE ADULT PLAYER

The role of the adult player is to guide the children into their own discoveries about the relationships between sounds and symbols. One word of caution: You must never drill letters or words for the child to memorize. The most important role of the adult player is to keep the spirit of discovery and fun alive.

It is crucial that you and your child regard playing these games as "playtime." If, one day, your child is interested in only one game, that's fine. It is more important for the child to enjoy playing than for you to accomplish an agenda. On the whole, I'd suggest a regular time of day for playing but no more than fifteen to twenty minutes a day.

READINESS GAMES

LEARNING SOUND NAMES OF LETTERS

TO BECOME good readers who can sound out words, independent of parent or teacher, children must be taught the sound names of the letters. When playing the readiness games, children will *not* use the alphabet names of the letters. Instead they will discover their sound names.

What does it mean to teach the sound names of the letters? For example, the sound of *a* in the word *apple* is /ă/, not /ay/. The sound of *m* at the beginning of the word *mitten* is /m/, not /em/. Pronouncing those sounds by their alphabet names, /ay/ or /em/, is confusing to children. The actual sounds they hear at the beginning of *apple* and *mitten* are quite different from the alphabet names of the letters.

In this book, a letter in slashes, for instance /m/, refers to the sound of the letter. The initial sound of *mitten* is clearly identifiable as /m/. A letter in italics, such as *m,* refers to the written form of the letter, which is also always referred to by its sound name.

Using the alphabet names in reading and spelling is usually a significant handicap for children. Children can sound out new words only if they know the sounds of the letters. Merely naming the letters "dee oh gee" does not enable them to read the word *dog*. Similarly, children who know the sound names of the letters can spell a word like *hat* by listening to themselves say /hat/ and recording the sounds they hear. They do not have to spell out the word *hat* by memorizing the meaningless sequence "aitch ay tee."

Although using the sound names of letters may seem strange at first to you, children will find it reasonable. They will accept that letters, just like people, have two names: The sound names are the "first names," and the alphabet names are the "last names." They are amused by the idea that letters, like children, should be called by their first names, not their last names.

It is true that many children will have picked up the alphabet names from blocks, books, and, of course, television shows like "Sesame Street." But if you, the adult, do not use the alphabet names in the games, their importance will fade into the background.*

THE LETTER-PICTURE DICTIONARY

LOWERCASE LETTERS

The letter-picture dictionary (see pp. 50–59) is the single most important tool for children learning sounds and letters. The dictionary contains each letter of the alphabet superimposed over a picture that elicits a spoken word beginning with that letter's sound name. For example, the letter *m* is superimposed over the picture of a mask.

The letter-picture dictionary is a self-teaching device that enables children to figure out sound-symbol relationships. The dictionary can be used by the children in two different ways. When the children know a letter but are unsure of its sound, they scan the letter pictures and locate the letter; they pronounce the name of the picture and identify its initial sound. Or, if the children can identify the sound of a letter but cannot recall how to form the letter—for example, the letter *f*—they can scan the letter-picture dictionary in search of a picture that starts with, in this case, /f/. When they locate *fan,* its

---

*These points are discussed in detail in my book *Get Ready to Read: A Practical Guide for Teaching Young Children at Home and in School* (New York: Walker and Company, 1991).

letter picture standing for /f/ enables them to discover the letter they want, *f*, which is superimposed on the picture. The first part of the letter-picture dictionary presents, in lowercase form, all letters of the alphabet, except *q*. The letter *q* is presented only in the digraph *qu*, along with three other very common digraphs: *sh, th*, and *ch*.

The letter-picture dictionary is an important teaching aid and should be easily accessible to the children. Encourage them to look up letters they are unsure of as you play the games.

LETTER SEQUENCE

The 28 sound-letter combinations presented in the readiness section are broken down into Sets A1 through A7. Six sets comprise four letters each; the seventh has four common digraphs. The letters are carefully sequenced so that look-alike letters or sound-alike letters are introduced as far apart as possible. For example, *m* is the first letter taught, while *n*, which children often confuse with *m*, is the eighth letter to be introduced.

Letters and sounds are introduced in the following sets:

A1 *m, f, l, a*
A2 *t, s, c, n*
A3 *i, h, p, r*
A4 *b, o, g, k*
A5 *e, d, j, u*
A6 *v, z, w, y*
A7 *qu, ch, th, sh*

(The letter *x* is not included here because there are no words familiar to children that begin with /x/. The letter *x* is introduced later in the reading games at the ends of known words such as *mix* or *box*.)

We suggest that you play the games with one set until the child fully masters all letters in the set before proceeding to the next one.

PICTURE CARDS

The picture cards (see pp. 60–77) are meant to elicit a specific, spoken word from the child for each picture. For instance, the picture of a man must be called "man" and not "face" or "daddy." The picture is intended to elicit a word that starts with /m/ and that can be matched to another picture that starts with /m/. Young children sometimes look at a picture such as an ambulance and call it a car or hospital car. In this case, the picture is meant to elicit a word that starts with the short *a*. Thus, *ambulance* is the correct word for use in the games. Therefore, it is important to discuss each picture with the children before you start playing a game. Make certain that they realize they must accept your name for the picture.

Only a few words in English begin with a short vowel sound that can be illustrated. Therefore, before you introduce a new set of sounds, glance through the pictures and set aside those pictures that may be unfamiliar. Then go over them with the children, naming each object and explaining its use. In this way, the children's speaking vocabulary is enlarged, and when they see these words in print later, they will know their meaning.

You can make certain of the proper vocabulary by consulting the following list. It is very important for the children to be familiar with any new word *before* they see its picture in a game.

NAMES OF PICTURE CARDS

SET A1

magnet matches mitten monkey mouse
fan feather fence fish fork
ladder leaf lemon lion lamb
ax ant anchor ambulance apple

Set A2

table toothbrush tiger tent turkey
sun sock scissors saw sandwich
coat candle cake cow camel
nurse nut net nest nail

Set A3

inch igloo ink infant insect
hammer horn horse hen hand
pig pan pie pencil pear
rake raccoon rope ring radio

Set A4

girl garage goat gum ghost
ostrich octopus orange ox otter
banana bell bat ball bed
key kitten king kangaroo kite

Set A5

egg engine elephant elf envelope
doughnut doll donkey dog door
jeep jacks jacket jet jar
umbrella (open) umbrella (closed) umpire

SET A6

vase vest violin vacuum valentine
zero zigzag zoo zipper zebra
wagon watch witch web window
yell yard (back) yard (school) yo-yo yarn

SET A7

shovel ship shower shell shoe
chair cherries chimney cheese chick
quail quarter question queen quilt
thistle thumb thorn thimble thermometer

LETTER CARDS

Using the letter cards (see pp. 78–95) is a more advanced step for children than using the letter-picture dictionary. It is a necessary step that enables children to recognize letters per se, without their pictorial context. The letter cards are also used in the card games that require both a picture and a letter card to complete a trick.

THE IMPORTANCE OF WRITING CORRECTLY

As the children play the readiness games, they will begin to learn how to hold a pencil and draw letters. It is important that these skills be taught properly, since it is far easier to correct a child early in the learning process than it is to correct habits later on.

Show the children how to hold a pencil between thumb and index finger while it rests against the third finger. Allow time for practice. The illustrations on pages 13 and 14 show how to teach children the sequential movement of pencil strokes in forming letters. Refer to these illustrations as often as necessary to be sure that your child is learning the correct sequence.

LOWERCASE LETTERS AND WRITING NAMES

Children as young as age three want to write their names. It is important that they learn to write their names in exactly the form they will use from first grade on: A name starts with a capital letter, while the rest is written in lowercase letters. This is the only capital letter they will learn at the very beginning when they start to play the readiness games. Each time a child wants to write his or her name, provide a model, and draw an arrow to show where to start each letter. Have young children trace their names repeatedly under your supervision. In this way, you can make sure they trace each letter from left to right and from top to bottom, habits that are best established early.

CAPITAL LETTERS

When children have mastered all the lowercase letters and before starting the reading games, introduce the capital letters. At the reading level, children will want to write names such as Dad or Nan, and they should learn to write all these names correctly.

These games purposefully introduce capital letters after the lowercase letters are learned. It is not advisable to introduce lowercase and capital letters at the same time, because it is difficult for children with poor visual memories to learn two forms for each letter. These children are never sure which form to use when they write words.

In the letter-picture dictionary you will find, after the lowercase letters, all the capital letters. Make new letter cards using capital letters and then play several of the readiness games that you used before with the lowercase letters. Using the letter-picture dictionary, at first, will be essential.

SEQUENTIAL MOVEMENT OF PENCIL STROKES IN FORMING LOWERCASE LETTERS

LETTER REVERSALS

The tracing games are especially suited for reinforcing the correct shape of a letter. For instance, most children have difficulty in distinguishing between the *b* and *d,* since they look alike to children for a long time. In persistent cases of *b* and *d* reversal, make the *b* solid (**b**), and explain that the *b* has a bell or ball in front. If necessary, you can make the *b* solid on all letter cards.

SEQUENTIAL MOVEMENT OF PENCIL STROKES IN FORMING CAPITAL LETTERS

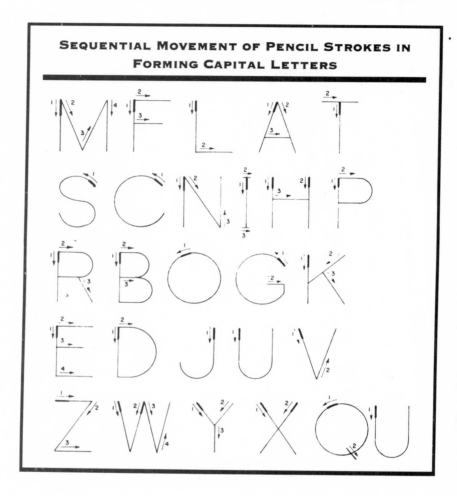

GETTING STARTED

As discussed earlier, the readiness games are designed to develop auditory discrimination and to enrich children's speaking vocabulary. Unless designated as solitaire or otherwise specified, all of the readiness games are designed to be played by two players, either an adult and a child or two children supervised by an adult. If more than two children want to play, make two teams. Pin green ribbons on one team and red ribbons on the other team. Each member gets a turn when her or his team is up. The first three games use the picture cards. Children will become familiar with the specific name of each picture. Then they will learn to listen to the initial sound of each word.

Play these games until the children can identify the initial sound of the name of each of the 20 picture cards in Set A1. You will see how their auditory discrimination improves after they have mastered the first set. Only then are they ready to discover how to record each sound by its letter.

Before reading about how to play these games, it will be helpful to have available the necessary materials listed in the Preparation section of each game. Directions on how to assemble these materials are on pages 43–45.

THE GAMES

PICK A CARD

PREPARATION.   From set A1, select three picture cards that start with /f/ and three with /m/. Place these six picture cards faceup before the children.

HOW TO PLAY.   First name each picture correctly, emphasizing its initial sound. Say, "This is a mitten; you hear the sound /m/ at its beginning." (Do not say /em/). Then explain to the child that you are going to ask for a certain picture card. You will not say its name, only the sound that starts its name. For instance, say, "Find a picture that starts with /f/." (Do not say /ef/). The child who finds an /f/ picture must tell you something about it and give the sound that starts its name. For instance, "It's a fan; it keeps you cool in the summer. It starts with /f/." She or he now keeps the picture card as a trick. The child with the most tricks wins.

RIDDLE GAME WITH PICTURES

PREPARATION.   From Set A1, select eight picture cards—two for each of the four sounds /m/, /f/, /l/, /a/. Place them on the table faceup.

HOW TO PLAY.   Explain that this time you are going to ask for a picture card by giving a riddle and the initial sound of the word. For example, say, "Give me the picture of something that tastes very sour. It starts with /l/." If the child you call on picks the picture of a lemon, the card is kept as a trick; if not, the card stays on the table.

It is important for every child to take the role of teacher while playing this game. As "teacher," the child selects a picture and identifies the initial sound. Young children will need help in asking even a simple riddle or in giving a description of the picture. Be sure they ask for a picture not only by giving a riddle but also by pronouncing its initial sound.

VARIATION: PARTNERS GAME

PREPARATION.   Put four or five picture cards from Set A1 on a tray, but have two that start with the same sound (e.g., lion, lollipop, mask, fork).

HOW TO PLAY.   Ask the children to say the name of each picture, listen to the initial sound, and then select the two that are partners because they both start with the same sound. Then let a child be the leader and *ask* for two pictures that are partners. All the players should get turns being the leader.

WHAT DID I TAKE AWAY?

PREPARATION.   From Set A1 select four picture cards, one for each sound. Place the cards faceup on a tray.

HOW TO PLAY. Ask the children to close their eyes while you take one picture card away. Suppose you remove the picture of the magnet. When they open their eyes, ask them to tell you which picture is missing. Encourage them to explain what a magnet is used for and to pronounce its initial sound, /m/.

LOTTO GAME WITH PICTURES

PREPARATION. It is easy to make this lotto game yourself. You will need enough 5″ × 8″ index cards to make one master card for each player. With a pencil, divide each index card into six equal spaces. Now photocopy the letter pictures from the letter-picture dictionary for *m, f, l,* and *a.* Paste one letter picture in the upper-left space of each index card. These will be the master cards. Take all picture cards for the four letters—five of each—and place them in a shuffled deck facedown.

HOW TO PLAY. A child is the caller. As she turns up each picture card, she names the picture and identifies the initial sound in *mitten* as /m/. The player who has the master card for /m/ claims the card with the mitten and fills one of his /m/ spaces. The first to fill all the spaces on the lotto card wins.

GAMES WITH THE LETTER-PICTURE DICTIONARY

Only after children have learned to identify the initial sounds of familiar words are they ready to learn to read the letter that represents each sound. You will notice that the letter-picture dictionary presents letters and sounds in a sequence that is not alphabetical. You should follow this sequence because letters that look alike (*b, d*) and sounds that are similar (/m/, /n/) are introduced as far apart as possible to avoid confusion. The first of such a pair is overlearned before the one it could be confused with is introduced.

Introduce each new letter by its letter picture. For instance, have the children name the first picture in the letter-picture dictionary: mask. Encourage them to emphasize the initial sound, /m/. Point out the letter *m* superimposed on the mask. Always refer to the printed letter *m* by using its sound, /m/.

The following games are played for the first time using only the letters *m* and *f* from Set A1. Introduce each letter with its letter picture, one at a time. Go on to the next letter only after each child has learned to identify the letter by its sound name (without referring to its letter picture).

PICTURE CARDS AND THE
LETTER-PICTURE DICTIONARY

PREPARATION.   Display the letter-picture dictionary. Take all the picture cards for *f* and *m* in Set A1. Shuffle and place the deck face-down.

HOW TO PLAY.   Have the child turn up the top picture, say its name, and identify its initial sound: *man,* /m/. He or she should locate the corresponding letter in the letter-picture dictionary. If there is some doubt, you can ask the child to listen once again: *Man* starts with the same sound as *mask.* The letter picture *mask* is covered by the corresponding picture card, *man.* Continue the game until the letter pictures for *mask* and *fan* have a pile of picture cards on top of them. The next time you play, add the picture cards for *l,* and after that for *a,* and so forth.

TRACING GAME USING THE
LETTER-PICTURE DICTIONARY

PREPARATION.   Take a sheet of tracing paper (or as many sheets as there are players) and fasten it to the first page of the letter-picture dictionary with tape, so the paper will not move. Now, with a thick piece of paper, cover up all the letters except *m, f,* and *l.* These three letters will be visible through the tracing paper.

HOW TO PLAY.   Say a word starting with /f/, perhaps *feather.* Call on a child (if there is more than one) and explain that one of the letter pictures also starts with the same sound, /f/. When the child finds *fan* have him or her trace the letter *f.* Say a word for each letter. Eventually, you might say a word beginning with another sound, but give the child fair warning that you will do so. In that case there will be no letter to trace.

VARIATION: USING A GRAB BAG

PREPARATION.   On notebook paper, outline in faint lines five *m*s and five *f*s. In a large paper bag collect ten corresponding toys or objects whose initial sounds begin with /m/ and /f/. As a child pulls out a toy, he or she says its name and identifies the initial sound of its name. This determines which letter should be traced. In case of doubt have the child use the letter-picture dictionary. If the children enjoy the Tracing Game, play it as often as once a day. Guide them while they write each letter, making certain each stroke is begun in the right place, drawn in the right direction, and written in the accepted sequence.

RACING GAME WITH THE STOP-AND-GO CUBE AND LETTER-PICTURE DICTIONARY

PREPARATION.   This game is best played with two to four children. Give each player a "man," or pawn. This can be a colored cube or tiny animal. Make a stop-and-go cube by coloring two faces of a wooden cube red (stop) and four faces green (go). Set out a photocopy of the first two lines of the letter-picture dictionary (p. 50).

HOW TO PLAY.   The course each player will run is as follows: Begin on the *m* square of the letter-picture dictionary and proceed from left to right across each row on the page. (This reinforces the direction, left to right, that the children will follow later when they begin to read.) Perhaps you should take the first turn to demonstrate the game. Toss the stop-and-go cube on the table. If it falls red side up, you lose your turn. If it falls green side up, you say, "Go," and move your pawn to the square with your first letter picture. The rule of the game is to say the letter picture's name and initial sound and the name of another word with the same initial sound; for example, *"Mask, /m/, mitten."* Then it is the next player's turn. If the cube falls with the green side up, the second player will join you on the first square. The first person to reach the *s* square is the winner.

As the children learn more letters, this game can be expanded to include all letters familiar to them. Children enjoy the Racing Game very much.

The most important function of the readiness games is to help children discover the relationship between sounds and symbols, that is, letters. For instance, the sound heard at the beginning of the word *mitten* is recorded as /m/. Knowing the relationship between sounds heard and the letters by which they are recorded is the key not only to reading but also to writing and spelling. The following are games for practicing sound-symbol relationships.

LETTER-WRITING GAME

PREPARATION.   When the children have become proficient in tracing letters, give each player a sheet of lined notebook paper and let them try writing letters freehand. If it is too difficult for a particular child, go back to the Tracing Game (p. 18).

HOW TO PLAY.   From Set A1, select ten picture cards for *m* and *f*. Shuffle them and place them facedown in front of the child. The child is to turn up a card, say the name of the picture, identify its initial sound, and then write the corresponding letter. Then it is the next player's turn. The player who has written five letters on a line has won.

VARIATION: LETTER-WRITING GAME USING A GRAB BAG

PREPARATION.   You can play the Letter-writing Game by placing toys corresponding to the picture cards for *m* and *f* in a grab bag. As a child pulls out a toy, he or she says its name and identifies its initial sound. The child then writes the corresponding letter.

MAKING A SOUND BOOK

PREPARATION.   For this activity, manila paper or inexpensive drawing paper is required.

HOW TO PLAY.   Draw two lines at the bottom of the paper and write the letter to be practiced, once on each line. The child is to write the letter, for example, *m,* on the two lines, then cut out from old magazines pictures that start with *m* and paste them onto the top of the sheet. On another day, the child can do an *f* page, and so on. When the child has several sheets, clip them together and make a cover out of construction paper. Let the child write her or his name on the cover and illustrate it.

MATCHING GAME

PREPARATION.   Select ten letter cards from Set A1, five for *m* and five for *f.* Select the ten corresponding picture cards and place all twenty cards together in one deck. Players should sit side by side.

HOW TO PLAY.   Shuffle the deck and place it facedown in the center of the table. The players take turns drawing one card at a time. Each picture card, as it is drawn, is placed faceup on the right side of the table and each letter card on the left. If a player turns up a picture of a fork, he or she pronounces its name and initial sound: *fork, /f/.* If there is a letter card for *f* on the table, a trick can be formed with the two cards. The player gets both cards and places them facedown. The player with the most tricks wins.

VARIATION

Show the children how to play the sorting game as solitaire. A picture card is matched with the corresponding letter card and the trick turned over. This form of solitaire is fun to play and gives added practice.

SNATCHING GAME

PREPARATION.   Select from Set A1 the five letter cards with *m* and the five with *f.* Shuffle the ten cards and place the deck in front of one player facedown. Now select the ten corresponding picture cards, shuffle them, and place the pile facedown in front of another player. The two players must sit side by side.

HOW TO PLAY.   Now both players turn up the top card of each pile simultaneously and watch carefully to see if the two cards match. The first person to see that a letter and a picture match yells out the sound name, snatches the other player's discard pile, and puts it and the two matching cards at the bottom of his playing pile. The player who gets all the cards wins.

Now play the last five games with the other two letters in Set A1, letters *l* and *a.*

BINGO GAME WITH LETTERS

PREPARATION.   This game is best played with two to four children. You will need one 5″ × 8″ index card for each player. With a pencil divide the cards into six equal spaces. Now photocopy the letter cards from Set A1. You will need six copies of each letter card.

Paste a letter card in each of the blank spaces on all the index cards. You will have to duplicate two of the letters on each bingo card (for example, *m, f, l, a, m, f*). Select the matching picture cards for *m, f, l,* and *a.* Place them in a shuffled deck facedown.

HOW TO PLAY.   A child is the caller. As a picture card is turned up, the child names the picture and identifies the initial sound—say, /m/. The child who has the letter *m* on the bingo card claims the picture card and puts it on the letter *m.* The first player to fill the bingo card wins.

BALL PITCHING GAME

PREPARATION.   Label three or four cardboard boxes with the latest letters the children know, using plain white paper and the letters without their letter pictures. Set the boxes in a row, and let the children take turns standing at a designated place, about eight to ten feet away. Provide a ball or a beanbag.

HOW TO PLAY.   When you say a word, for instance, *apple,* a child has to identify the initial sound out loud, then throw the ball into the correct box, in this case the /a/ box.

GO FISH

PREPARATION.   From Set A1 remove all twenty letter cards, five each of *m, f, l,* and *a,* and the twenty matching picture cards. Shuffle these forty cards and deal six to each player. Place the rest of the cards in a central pile facedown.

HOW TO PLAY.   The players begin scanning their cards in search of a trick made up of a picture card and its matching letter card. If the first player has no tricks, she looks at one of the unmatched letter cards, for example, the letter card *f,* and asks another player, "Do you have a picture card that begins with /f/?" If the other player has a picture card for /f/, he gives it to the child, who then makes a trick and also can ask for another card. But if the person asked has no picture card, he replies, "Go fish." This means the first player must draw a card from the central deck. The player who has the most tricks wins.

This game can be used as a test. Only when the children are able to say the sound name of every letter in Set A1 should you go on to the next set of letters, in Sets A2, A3, and so on.

CONCENTRATION

PREPARATION.   From Set A1, select three letter cards and three matching picture cards for *m*. Do the same for *f*. Arrange these twelve cards facedown on the table.

HOW TO PLAY.   The first player turns up one card. If it is a picture, the child pronounces its name and initial sound and then tries to locate a matching letter card. If she selects a letter card that does not match, both cards must be turned facedown. It will help all players if the cards are kept in their original positions. The players should try to memorize the exact position of each card in case one or the other is needed for the next turn. On the other hand, if the cards do match, a trick has been made and the player can pick it up; this entitles the player to another turn. As the children become more competent, you may use more letters, but never let the game become too difficult; twelve or sixteen cards in all make for a good game.

This game also tests the knowledge of sound-symbol relationships. Children should master letters in Set A1 before learning more letters.

All of the preceding games should be played and mastered by the children, progressing from Set A1 through Set A7. Only after all the lowercase letters in A1 are learned and the children have become familiar with the letters in capital form should you proceed to the reading games.

READING GAMES

THE READING games build on the skills learned through the readiness games. These games have been carefully designed to teach children to read printed words accurately and to put them back into the familiar spoken language. At the same time, children learn to write these words accurately. Thus, through playing these games, children build the foundation for fluent reading and accurate spelling. Here again, as in the readiness games, children identify letters by their sound names. The reading vocabulary that we use in the games contains only words that are spelled exactly the way they sound.

What is meant by "read" in this book is altogether different from the parroting that results from flash card drills, where students may end up "reading" m-a-n as *father* or c-a-b as *truck*. For a variety of reasons, drilling preschool children on what words say in a book does not result in a solid reading foundation. Children do not enjoy memorizing words, nor does memorization allow them to discover new words on their own.

Included here are twenty reading games that enable children to read and write approximately 150 phonetically regular words, that is, words in which each letter represents the same sound learned previously. In the process of playing the games, children learn the actual reading and writing of words. They gain a true understanding of the relationships between letters and their sounds, and this gives them a solid foundation for learning to read and write more words than are included here. Consequently, children not only gain satisfaction from learning to read but they also develop an ever-increasing confidence in their ability to learn and think.

These reading games introduce a new phase of learning. Here, children no longer concentrate on initial sounds but instead listen to the structure of familiar spoken words that have been broken into two component parts. Through playing these games, the children will learn the word *man*, for example, which has been separated into the main part, /ma/, and the ending, /n/. The children learn to rejoin the parts to form the familiar word *man*. At this stage, monosyllabic words are used in which each sound is recorded by one letter. Children begin the reading games by mastering a few words, such as *man, cat,* or *pad* (Set B1). They find they can easily transfer these skills to the reading of words of the same pattern, such as *mad* or *sad,* which they have never seen before—a heady, delightful way of finding out they can read on their own without any help from an adult. Reading the main part, for example /ma/, as a unit gives children a boost in learning to read fluently and with comprehension. Children are thus able to avoid the pitfall of trying to blend three separate sounds, /m-a-n/, which is a step of such difficulty that it often hinders fluency and interferes with comprehension.

One of the components of the reading games is special dominoes. On one set is the main part of words—*ca, ma,* or *ha.* The second set provides the appropriate endings—*b, n,* or *t,* for example. Word games with the dominoes result in reading the main part of a word as *one* unit.

STRESSING COMPREHENSION

From the very beginning, children develop a keen understanding that reading consists of both decoding (or sounding out) and comprehension. Immediately after having a child read a word, ask her to tell you what the word means or to tell you something about the word. ("Cat!

It's an animal that says meow. I wish we had a cat.") In this way, children put the words they read back into the more familiar spoken language, proving that they have understood its meaning. Reading with comprehension should be checked and stressed at every level.

GUESSING

Children should never be encouraged to guess at a word. From the very beginning, these games guide children to the realization that while the picture can be that of a cat or a kitten, the word can only stand for one thing: a cat. Guessing may not be harmful to children in first, second, or third grade, but by fourth grade, a math problem can easily be misunderstood if a child reads "a" for "the." It is inexcusable to teach children guessing skills in first or second or third grade, because they will have to unlearn them painstakingly by the time they reach fourth grade. Better to develop skills on which they can rely throughout school.

SHADING AND STRUCTURE OF WORDS

Shading is used on many of the components to aid visual discrimination of consonant and vowel sounds. This accentuates the structure of the word. In the reading games, each word consists of a gray vowel preceded and followed by a black consonant (or consonants). The gray vowel reminds the children that the vowel sound in each word group is the same.

Children may ask why some letters are gray. Give them the simple explanation that the gray letters are vowels, the most important letters in the alphabet. No word can be pronounced without a vowel sound. Do not expect young children to remember the name *vowel* or *consonant*. Remembering these terms serves no purpose at this stage.

Motor Skills

If the children you teach have difficulty with fine motor coordination, try pasting the cardboard letters on a set of real dominoes. The real dominoes are much easier for children to handle.

Getting Started

In the games that follow, children not only learn to read actual words but they also discover, on their own, how to read similar words. This increases their joy in playing the reading games, some of which are versions of old-time favorite card games. Unless designated as solitaire or otherwise specified, all of the reading games are designed to be played by two players, either an adult and a child or two children supervised by an adult. If more than two children want to play, make two teams. Pin green ribbons on one team and red ribbons on the other team. Each member gets a turn when her/his team is up.

Throughout the readiness stage children were taught to focus on the initial sound of a word. Now, at the reading stage, they are taught to break monosyllabic words like *hat* into a main part, *ha,* and an ending, *t.* Children taught to read *ma, ca,* and *ha* only need to use one-step blending, for example, *ca* and *t (cat).* This eliminates the tedious, old-fashioned procedure of blending *c-a-t.* The first game, the Riddle Game, prepares children for this transition on the spoken level. Once this foundation has been built, it will be easier for them to decode printed words.

Play all the games that follow using only the vocabulary of Set B1, which contains short-*a* words. Do not move on to the short-*i* words in B2 until the children have mastered the new skills necessary for reading these fifteen short-*a* words. When the children can read them fluently and without hesitation, introduce the short-*i* words in B2.

The last two games in this section, Concentration and the List Game, can be used to test children's reading fluency before introducing the next set of words.

After the children have mastered the words in one set, go on to the next set. Once the children have learned to read, write, and spell the short-*i* words (Set B2), play their favorite games mixing short-a and short-*i* words. As children progress through the games, you can make the games very exciting by using five card pairs from each set.*

Before reading about how to play these games, it will be helpful to have available the necessary materials listed in the Preparation section of each game. Directions on how to assemble these materials are on pages 96–99.

THE GAMES

RIDDLE GAME
(PREPARATORY GAME, SPOKEN LEVEL)

PREPARATION.   Select any six picture cards from words in Set B1. Place them before two children.

HOW TO PLAY.   Pronounce the name of one of the pictures by breaking the word into two parts. Ask, "Which picture do I mean if I say /ha t/?" Before they can find the picture, the children must put the two pieces they heard back together again. They will say /hat/ as soon as they realize how the parts sound together. The player who first points to the picture claims it as his or her own.

Each player should have a turn being the teacher; it is important that a child be able to break a word into two parts at this stage.

WORD-BUILDING GAMES

It is sensible to use only regular words at this beginning reading stage. That way the children are introduced only to short *a* words like *cat,*

---

*When children can read all the words taught in Sets B1 through B5 and still want to "read more," you may want to acquire my book *Get Ready to Read: A Practical Guide for Teaching Young Children at Home and in School* (New York: Walker and Company, 1991). It describes additional games and also introduces sentence reading.

man, or *hat.* The children become well acquainted with the structure of these words because it is reinforced by building the words with dominoes (pp. 104–113). If the children then encounter a new *a* word, they will be able to read it on their own.

Reading and Building Words

Preparation.   Select the five word-picture cards for *man, hat, cat, pan,* and *fan* of Set B1 (the short-*a* group).

Help the children identify each picture correctly, and explain that they must accept your name for the picture, because each picture stands for a certain word with a certain sound. ("This is a cat, not a kitten.") The children pronounce the name of the picture *cat.* Now they read the word printed below it, /ca t/. They probably will read it in two parts, /ca t/. Ask them to read the word again and then tell you what it means. This time they should read the word fluently, in one piece. "Cat! It's an animal that meows." In this way, the children put the word they have read back into the spoken language, proving they have understood its meaning.

How to play.   When the children have read all five words, turn the word-picture cards over. Get the picture cards and the word dominoes for the words just introduced. Arrange the main-part dominoes facedown above the pictures and the ending dominoes along the right side. Ask the children to turn up a main-part domino and read it aloud in one flow. Suppose the domino is *pa.* It is to be read as a unit, /pa/, not /p/ + /a/. The child is now to scan the pictures to discover which picture begins with /pa/. The picture of the pan might be selected and the domino placed below the picture. Encourage the player to say the word again, /pan/, this time listening for its final sound. He or she hears /n/ and searches for the *n* domino to complete the word. The whole word, /pan/, is then read. Have the children build each word below its word-picture card. (This is good practice for spelling. It helps with the thinking part of spelling without requiring the additional task of writing the letters.) At the end of the game, turn the word-picture cards over so the children can check the spelling of the words they have built. For the next few days, play this game by adding three new words a day, or more if the children really want them. When the children can read all fifteen words, they are ready for the next game.

CAN YOU BUILD THIS WORD?

PREPARATION.   This game is best played by two to four children. Select eight picture cards and the corresponding word dominoes for the main parts and endings of Set B1. Place several cards before each player. Turn the main-part dominoes facedown and divide them among the players. Place all the domino endings faceup in a common pool at the side of the table.

HOW TO PLAY.   A player picks up a main-part domino, reads it as a unit, for example /ca/, and looks for a picture that begins with /ca/. If the player holds a picture of, for example, a can, the *ca* domino is placed below the picture. The child then pronounces the whole word, /can/, listening for the final sound, /n/, and hunts among the endings for the *n* domino to complete the word. If the player has no picture for a word beginning with /ca/, he gives up the domino to the next player, who then builds the word under her picture, if she has it.

After all the words have been built, you can call them back by playing another game. Call for a domino word by giving a simple definition or asking a riddle, "What goes on your head? It starts with /ha/." The player must scan all the words he has built to locate *hat*.

VARIATION

Shuffle the picture cards and place them facedown in a pile in the center of the table. Divide the main-part dominoes among the players and turn them faceup. Place the domino endings faceup along the side of the table in a common pool.

HOW TO PLAY. The first player picks up a picture card and identifies it, for example, /pan/. He or she puts the card on the table and scans the main-part dominoes. If the player has the *pa* domino, it is placed below the word-picture card and completed with the correct ending to form *pan*. If the player does not have the *pa* domino, the picture card of *pan* must be put at the bottom of the pile. The player who can build the most words wins.

WORD DOMINO GAME WITH THE STOP-AND-GO CUBE

PREPARATION. Use the stop-and-go cube you made for the readiness games (see p. 19) and all the dominoes from set B1. Put a tray on the table for discarded dominoes. Place the main-part dominoes facedown and divide them among the players. Arrange the word endings faceup along the sides of the table.

HOW TO PLAY. The player throws the cube. If it lands green side up, she can pick up a domino, read it, and then look for an ending that will transform it into a meaningful word. Suppose *ca* is drawn and the player selects *t* to form the word *cat*. The child must read it to you and tell you about it.

The players keep the dominoes for the words they build. The game continues until the dominoes have been used up. The player who has built the most words is the winner. Toward the end of the game, a player may not be able to use a main-part domino; it is then placed in the tray.

BUILDING WORDS WITH DOMINOES

PREPARATION. Cut manila folders in half and give one part to each player. From words in Set B1, select picture cards and arrange six of them three to a row faceup on each player's half folder. Put the corresponding main-part dominoes facedown, in a row above the cards, and arrange the endings faceup at the sides of the folders.

How to play. Call on a child to turn up a main-part domino and name it. Then comes the excitement. Who of the players can first claim it for one of the pictures on his lotto card? Whoever has claimed the main part now looks for the proper ending to complete the word. The player who has first built all the words on her lotto card wins.

Many children enjoy playing this game as solitaire. In this case, arrange six picture cards on each folder. Let the child build the words for the pictures on all the cards.

Playing this game is a good way to find out whether the children have mastered the words of the short-*a* group. This group will take the longest time. Then move on to the short-*i* group of words, Set B2. Do not rush, for it is more important that the children enjoy these games than that you reach your desired goals.

WRITING GAMES

The children already know how to write single letters. They know how to build these words with the dominoes. Now they are ready to play the first tracing and writing games. Writing words is the logical counterpart to reading words. It is exciting for children to discover that they can write words as naturally as they learned to read them.

However, the mechanics of aligning letters properly is difficult for most children. Therefore, it is advisable to play the next two tracing games as preparation for writing words freehand.

CAN YOU MAKE A WORD?

Preparation. This game is best played with two children; if there are more than two players, prepare additional pieces of notebook paper. Take the word-picture cards from Set B1. On notebook paper, write the main parts of six of the short-*a* words, for example, *ma, ha, ca, pa, fa, ba,* in light lines and give it to the first player. On another piece of paper, also write the main parts of different short-*a* words, for example, *ja, na, ga, ca, ma, ba,* and give it to the second player. Place the word-picture cards facedown in a pile between the players.

How to play.   The first player picks up a word-picture card, reads it, and puts the card to the side, facedown. He then scans his sheet to see if he has the main part of that word. If he has, he traces the main part and then adds the proper ending of his own and keeps the card. If he does not have the main part, he puts the card at the bottom of the pile, and the next player gets a turn picking up a word-picture card. The game ends when one player has a complete set of words on her paper. At that point, each player can turn up all his word-picture cards and check the spelling of his words against those on his cards.

V A R I A T I O N

Here, too, children enjoy playing this game as solitaire. Print ten of the main parts of short-*a* words and give the child the whole deck of short-*a* word-picture cards from Set B1. He will be able to write some words, but he will also turn up cards whose beginnings are not on his paper. This will add suspense.

TRACING GAME WITH PICTURE CARDS

Preparation.   Print a list of words from Set B1 in very light lines. Use a blank sheet for yourself or let it be a game of solitaire. Make a pile of corresponding picture cards. Use the stop-and-go cube to indicate when each player may write a word.

How to play.   The players take turns drawing a picture card and naming the picture and then tossing the stop-and-go cube to see if they will be allowed to write it. If the cube lands green side up, the word may be traced. But if the cube is red, it goes to the next player. The game is finished when one list of ten words has been completed.

LATER ADVANCED VERSION

Instead of tracing the words, let the children play this game by writing freehand on lined notebook paper.

WORD PICTURE CARDS AND TRACING WORDS

PREPARATION.   On paper, print seven short-*a* words in very light lines and give the sheet to the first player. Print seven different short-*a* words on another paper in light lines and give it to the second player. (Prepare additional sheets for additional players.) Now shuffle the word-picture cards from Set B1 and place them facedown.

HOW TO PLAY.   The first player picks up a word-picture card, reads it, and then scans the words on her paper to see if she has that particular word. If she has it, she can trace the word. If she does not, the word-picture card goes to the bottom of the pile. It is then her partner's turn. The player who has traced all her words has won.

VARIATION

Many children have enjoyed this game as solitaire. They enjoy timing themselves with a kitchen timer or stopwatch. Each time they check if their time improved, and they can see their progress from week to week.

WORD PICTURE CARDS AND WRITING WORDS

PREPARATION.   Select six word-picture cards from Set B1 and put them faceup in a row in front of the children. Give each child a ruled sheet and a folder and have them write their names on the folders. These will be their very first writing books. Anytime a writing game is played, each child puts the sheet in his or her folder.

How to play.   Have one child read the first card and then turn it facedown. Now have the child write the word from memory. The players should read the word back to themselves and then check the spelling with the word-picture card.

Can You Build or Write These Words in the Correct Order?

Preparation.   Select three word-picture cards from Set B1 and the corresponding word dominoes for the main parts and endings. Place the cards in a row on the table; for instance: *cat, nap, hat.*

How to play.   Have the children read the words and then turn the cards over. Ask the children if they can remember what the first word was. Call on someone to build it below the first turned-over card with the dominoes and call on others to continue by building the next two words in their proper sequence. To check, the word-picture cards are turned faceup again. When the children have played this game for quite a while, you and they may decide to add a fourth word-picture card. The added challenge provides continued zest for playing.

Variation

Give the children lined notebook paper. Ask a child to turn the three word-picture cards facedown and write the words in their correct sequence. Each time, turn up the word-picture cards as a check for spelling and sequence.

WRITING GAME WITH THE STOP-AND-GO CUBE

PREPARATION.   From Set B1, select eight word-picture cards and place them faceup on the table. Get the stop-and-go cube and give each player a ruled sheet of paper.

HOW TO PLAY.   The first player throws the stop-and-go cube. If it lands with red on top, the cube passes to the next player. If green is on top, the child can write a word that you dictate. Choose any one of the word-picture cards before you. After glancing at the word, the child turns the card over and writes the word from memory. Take turns until one of the players has managed to write down five words and thus wins the game.

WRITING GAME WITH TOYS

PREPARATION.   Prepare sheets of paper by drawing sets of four horizontal lines, leaving ample space between the sets. Collect in a large paper bag toys or objects whose names represent short-*a* words, for example, a fan, pad, bag, hat, cap, cat, map, can, jam, and rag.

HOW TO PLAY.   Give the children the prepared sheets of paper. Have them shut their eyes and touch a toy or object from the bag. Let them guess what it is, open their eyes, and take the toy out to check if they are right. Then ask them to record its name on the paper.

RHYMING GAME WITH WORD CARDS

PREPARATION.   Play a rhyming game with the children. Explain that two words rhyme when they sound alike (for example, *cat* and *pat*). Now say a word, for example, *nap,* and let the children think of a rhyming word. If necessary, give a hint, for example, "It is something you wear on your head" (cap). Play the rhyming game until the children realize that two words rhyme when the middle and end of the word are the same but that the beginning will be different. Cut eight lined index cards (3″ × 5″) in half and divide them between two players. Now shuffle the word cards from Set B1 and place them facedown in a pile in the center of the table.

HOW TO PLAY.   The first player picks up a word card and reads the word. If he can think of a rhyming word, he writes it on his index card and claims the word card as a trick. Now the next player gets a turn. The player who has the most tricks wins.

VARIATION

Children enjoy making their own rhyming books. Provide the children with lined paper and the word cards. As they pick up a word card, they draw a picture of that word and then write as many rhyming words underneath as they can think of. When they have several sheets, clip them together and make a cover out of two pieces of construction paper. Let the children write their names on it and illustrate the cover.

PRACTICING FLUENT READING

As you know, beginning readers learn to read by first sounding out single words such as *ma-n* or *ca-t*. While the blending process is essential for beginning readers, good readers need to go beyond it. If, for instance, children read *Da-d ha-s a ha-t,* they cannot comprehend the meaning of the whole sentence. Good readers need to learn to read words at a glance, i.e., fluently. Only when children have learned to read words fluently will they be able to comprehend the meaning of sentences. Fluency is achieved through practice, which will be provided in the games that follow.

WORD LOTTO

PREPARATION.   This game is excellent for practicing scanning and reading words fluently and quickly. Select twelve word cards and corresponding picture cards from Set B1.

HOW TO PLAY.   Deal each player six word cards. Help the children arrange three of the cards to form a horizontal row; the next three cards should be placed directly below the first row. This is called a lotto formation. Now shuffle the corresponding twelve picture cards and place them facedown in a pile. Call on a child to be the caller. She draws a picture card from the deck and says its name. (For example, *cat*). Whoever has the corresponding word card can claim the picture card and cover her word with it. The winner is the first person who covers all the word cards with pictures.

PICTURE LOTTO WITH WORD CARDS

This is the opposite of Word Lotto. This time, place the picture cards in a lotto formation and use the word cards in the central deck.

HOW TO PLAY.   The caller reads a word card and the players scan the pictures for the one that corresponds to it. The winner is the one who first covers all the picture cards with words.

VARIATION

As a putting-away game, a new, interesting task can be posed. You may give a very simple riddle, and the child must find the answer by scanning all her words. For instance, "I am thinking of something you hit a ball with." If a child is having trouble, you say, "It starts with /ba/." Whoever finds the word *bat* gives you both word and picture cards to put away. The game ends when there are no more cards.

THE MATCHING GAME

PREPARATION.   Begin with Set B1. Take the fifteen picture cards and the corresponding word cards for the short-*a* words. Shuffle the thirty cards together and place them facedown in a pile.

HOW TO PLAY.   The first player turns up a card, for instance, the picture of a man. The next player perhaps picks up a card with the word *cat* on it. If another player now picks up the picture card for *cat,* he can match the word card *cat* and take the two cards and form a trick. If the card had been the word *man,* he could have taken the picture card of *man* and also had a trick. When no cards in a play can be paired, they are put at the bottom of the pile. The player with the most tricks is the winner.

V A R I A T I O N

This game can also be played alone. Shuffle the cards and place them facedown. As the child turns up a picture card, it is put on the left side of the table; word cards are put on the right. Whenever two cards match, they are paired as a trick.

GO FISH

PREPARATION.   Shuffle the fifteen picture cards and fifteen matching word cards from Set B1 and deal each player six. Place the rest in a central pile facedown.

HOW TO PLAY.   Suppose the first player has the word card for *cat.* He asks his partner for the picture card of *cat.* If the partner doesn't have it, she says, "Go fish." The first player then picks up a card from the deck. If he draws the picture card of the cat, he has a trick and puts it down in front of him. Now it is the second player's turn to ask for a card. The player who has the most tricks wins.

SNATCHING GAME

PREPARATION.   From Set B1, use the deck of picture cards and the deck of matching word cards.

HOW TO PLAY.   Shuffle the word cards and put them facedown in front of one child. Shuffle the picture cards and put them facedown in front of the other child. Now both children simultaneously turn up the top card, watching carefully to see if the two cards match. The first child to see that a word and picture match, yells out the word, snatches the other player's card, and claims the trick. The player who has more tricks wins.

CONCENTRATION

PREPARATION.   From Set B1, select six word cards and six matching picture cards. Shuffle the cards, and then arrange them facedown on the table in three rows.

HOW TO PLAY.   The first player turns up two cards from any of the three rows. If they match, they form a trick. If they do not, they are turned facedown. The players try to remember the identity and position of each card that has been turned up. The next player turns up one card. She may remember two of the previously turned-over cards. One of them may be the needed match. In this case, if she has remembered correctly the player turns it up again and gains a trick, which carries with it the privilege of taking another turn. If they do not make a correct match, they are both turned facedown in their original places. This is very good for children who need more practice to sharpen visual memory and spatial orientation.

LIST GAME

PREPARATION.   On a sheet of paper, print a different list of ten words from Set B1 for each player, but make sure there are several words in common. Select corresponding word cards, shuffle, and place them in a deck facedown.

HOW TO PLAY. The players take turns drawing a card, reading the word aloud, then scanning his or her own list for it. If the word is on the list, it is crossed off; if not, the word card is placed at the bottom of the deck. The player who is first to cross off all the words on his or her list is the winner.

MATERIALS FOR THE READINESS GAMES

COMPONENTS OF READINESS GAMES

Letter-Picture Dictionary
140 Picture Cards
140 Letter Cards

The picture cards and letter cards are divided into seven sets (A1, A2, and so on). Each set contains 20 picture and 20 letter cards.

ASSEMBLING THE COMPONENTS OF READINESS GAMES

The following pages contain all the materials necessary for assembling the component parts of the readiness games. These pages are designed to be photocopied onto 8½" × 11" paper, two book pages per photocopy, leaving the back of each photocopied sheet blank. With photocopies of the component parts, it is very easy for you to make all the games. All you will need is glue, a package of blank 3"

X 5″ index cards, ten blank 5″ X 8″ index cards, seven 9″ X 6″ manila envelopes or 11½″ X 12½″ plastic food bags, and twelve manila folders.

Older children and grandparents will enjoy helping you to assemble the readiness games.

LETTER-PICTURE DICTIONARY

This dictionary (pp. 50–59) is a self-teaching device that helps children figure out sound-symbol relationships. It is important to keep the dictionary handy, within reach of the children. I recommend photocopying the dictionary twice and pasting each set of pages onto manila folders, which can then be set up as displays in front of the children.

Make sure the capital letters are on separate folders, and use them only after the lowercase letters have been mastered.

PICTURE CARDS

1. Photocopy pp. 60–77, and cut pictures apart along lines indicated.

2. Mount pictures onto index cards.

3. Stack pictures into seven decks according to the set number (A1, A2, and so on) and wrap each deck with a rubber band.

LETTER CARDS

1. Photocopy pp. 78–95, and cut letters apart along lines indicated.

2. Paste letters onto index cards.

3. Stack the letter cards into seven decks, according to the set number (A1, A2, and so on) and wrap each deck with a rubber band.

After making the picture cards and letter cards, organize them by assembling storage envelopes as described in the following steps.

1. Label each of seven 9″ × 6″ envelopes using one of the labels provided on pp. 46–49 (Set A1, Set A2, and so on).

2. Locate your picture cards for Set A1 (pp. 60–62). There are a total of twenty picture cards, five pictures for each of the four letters introduced in the set.

3. Locate your letter cards for Set A1 (pp. 78–80). There are five letter cards for each letter introduced in the set, making a total of twenty letter cards.

4. Put the deck of picture cards and the deck of letter cards from Set A1 into the 9″ × 6″ envelope labeled for Set A1.

5. Repeat steps 3 and 4 for Sets A2 through A7.

LABELS FOR THE READINESS GAMES

The labels on pp. 46–49 may be photocopied and pasted onto 9″ × 6″ envelopes, which can be used to store the materials for each set. Note that the labels provide a summary of the contents of each set.

Set A1

m f l a

20 Picture Cards

magnet matches mitten monkey mouse

fan feather fence fish fork

ladder leaf lemon lion lamb

ax ant anchor ambulance apple

20 Letter Cards

Set A2

t s c n

20 Picture Cards

table toothbrush tiger tent turkey

sun sock scissors saw sandwich

coat candle cake cow camel

nurse nut net nest nail

20 Letter Cards

SET A3

i h p r

20 PICTURE CARDS

inch igloo infant ink insect

hammer horn horse hen hand

pig pan pie pencil pear

rake raccoon rope ring radio

20 LETTER CARDS

SET A4

b o g k

20 PICTURE CARDS

banana bell bat ball bed

ostrich octopus orange ox otter

girl garage goat gum ghost

key kitten king kangaroo kite

20 LETTER CARDS

SET A5

e d j u

20 PICTURE CARDS

egg engine elephant elf envelope
doughnut doll donkey dog door
jeep jacks jacket jet jar
umbrella (open) umpire umbrella (open)
umbrella (closed) umpire

20 LETTER CARDS

SET A6

v z w y

20 PICTURE CARDS

vase vest violin vacuum valentine
zero zigzag zoo zipper zebra
wagon watch witch web window
yell yard (backyard) yard (schoolyard)
yoyo yarn

20 LETTER CARDS

SET A7

qu ch th sh

20 PICTURE CARDS

quail quarter question queen quilt
chair cherries chimney cheese chick
thistle thumb thorn thimble thermometer
shovel ship shower shell shoe

20 LETTER CARDS

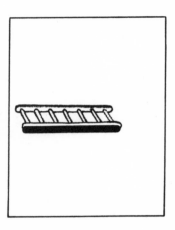

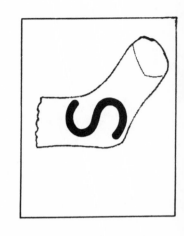

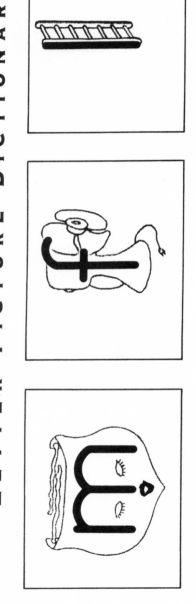

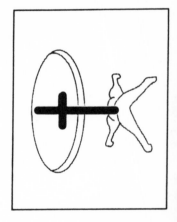

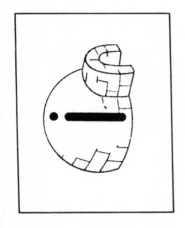

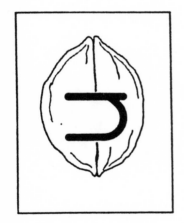

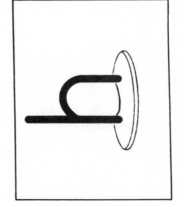

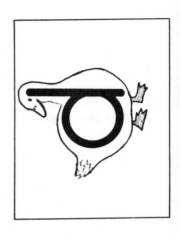

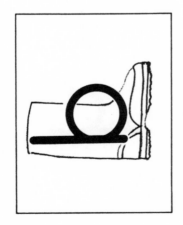

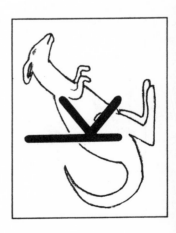

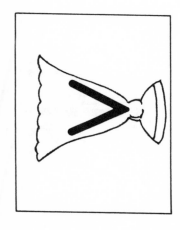

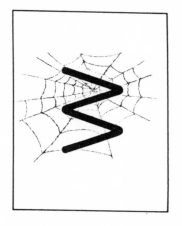

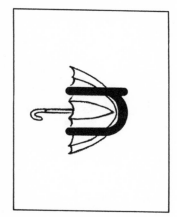

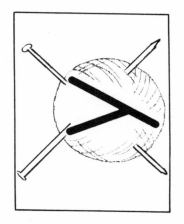

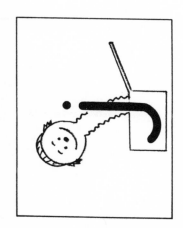

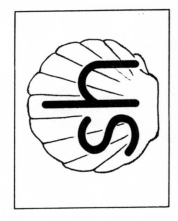

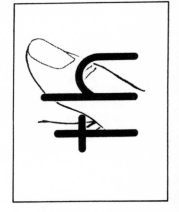

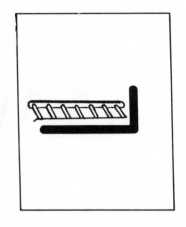
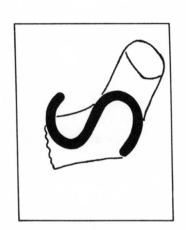
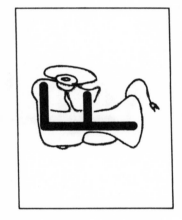

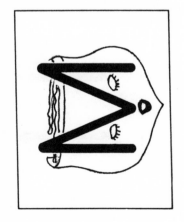

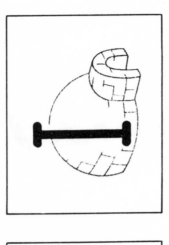

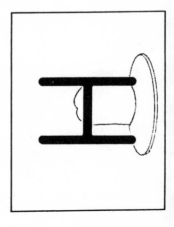

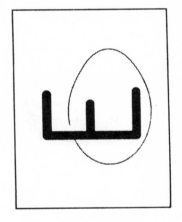

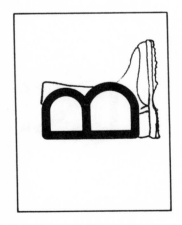

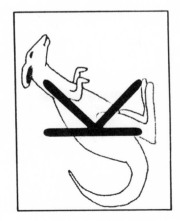

57

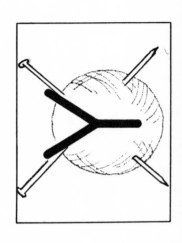

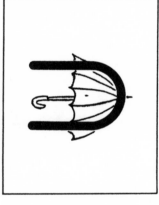

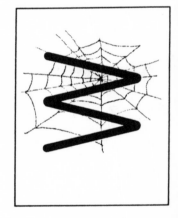

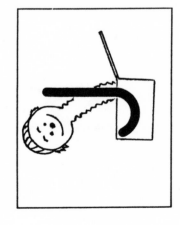

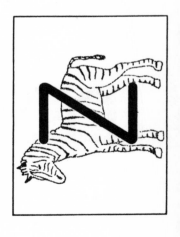

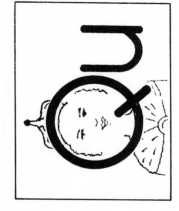

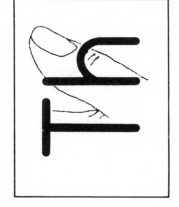

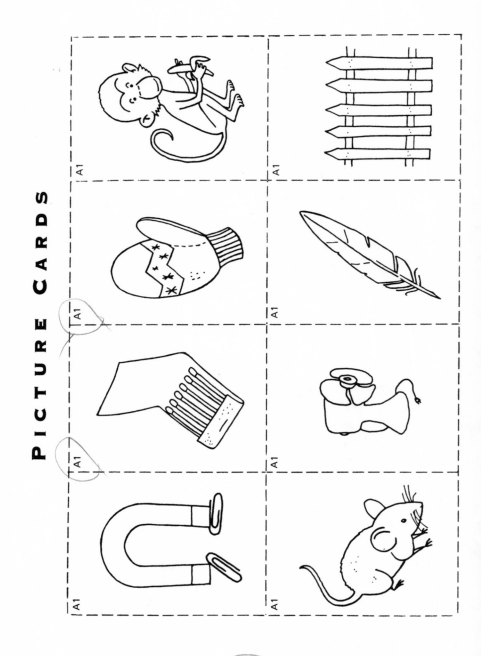

A1

A1

A1

A1

A1

A1

A1

A1

Picture Cards

A1

A1

A1

A1

A2

A2

A2

A2

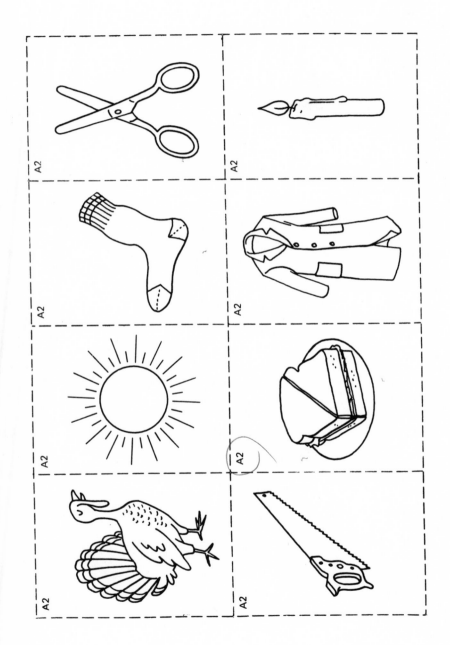

A.2

A.2

A.2

A.2

A.2

A.2

A.2

A.2

PICTURE CARDS

A2
A2
A2
A2
A2
A2
A2
A2

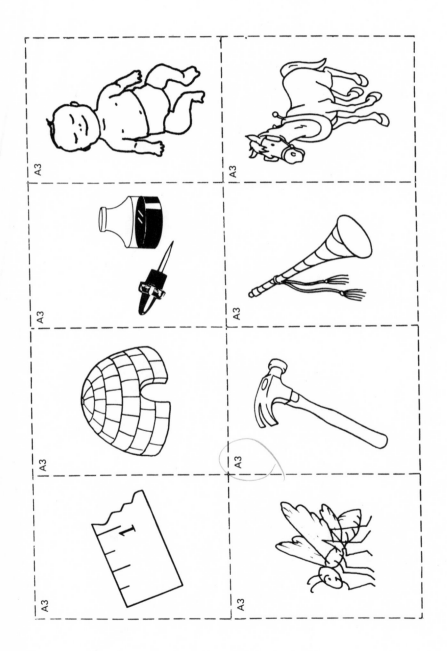

A3

A3

A3

A3

A3

A3

A3

A3

A3

A3

A3

A3

A3

A3

A3

A3

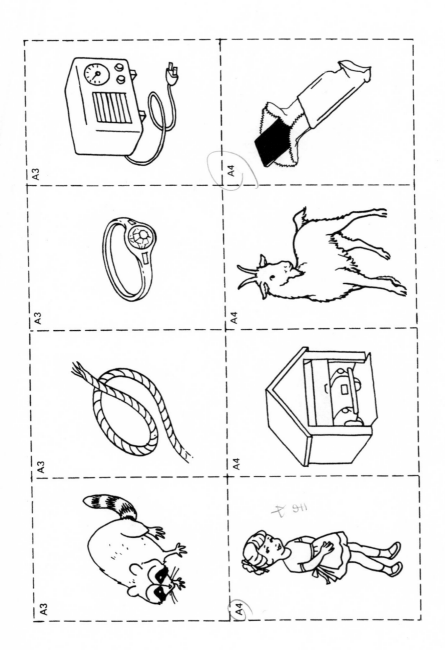

A3

A4

A3

A4

A3

A4

A3

A4

67

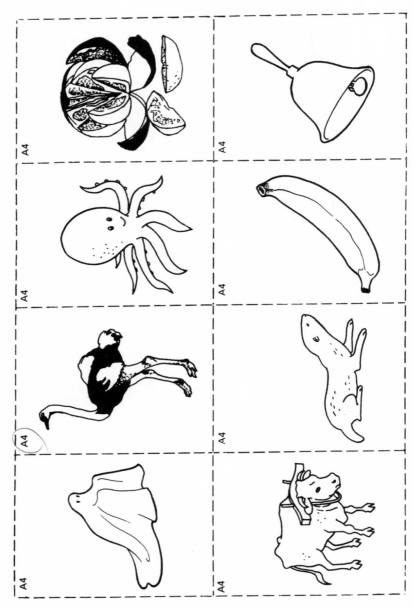

A4

A4

A4

A4

A4

A4

A4

A4

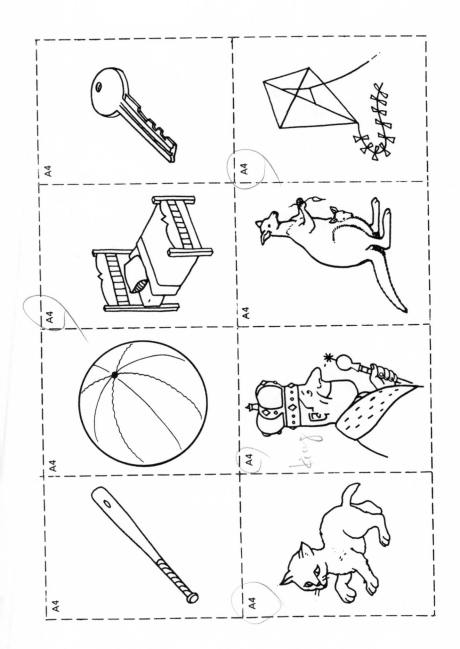

PICTURE CARDS

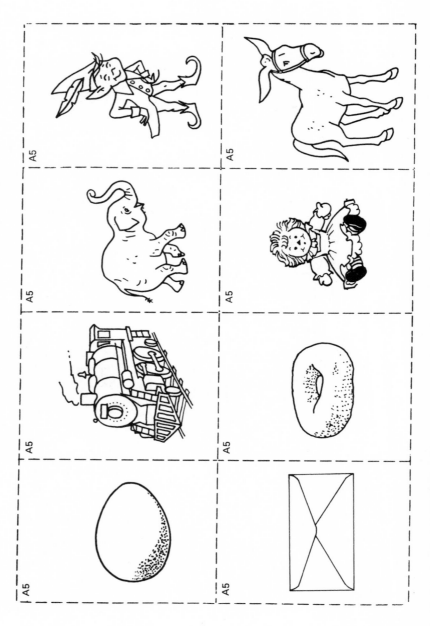

A5

A5

A5

A5

A6

A6

A6

A6

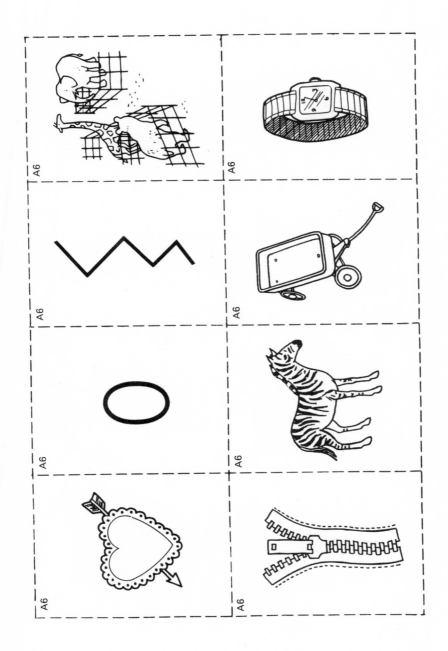

PICTURE CARDS

A6

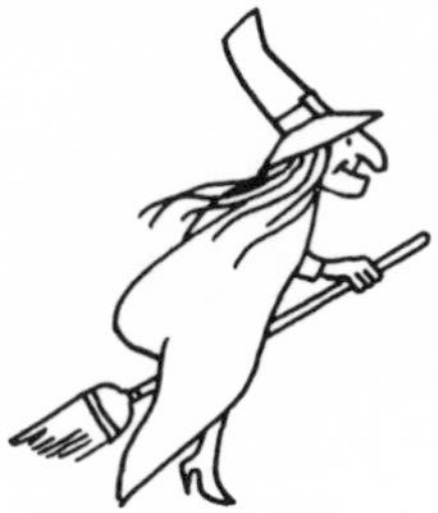

A6

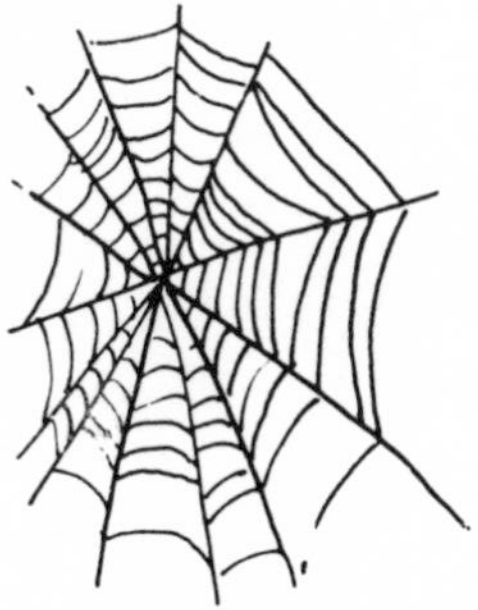

A6

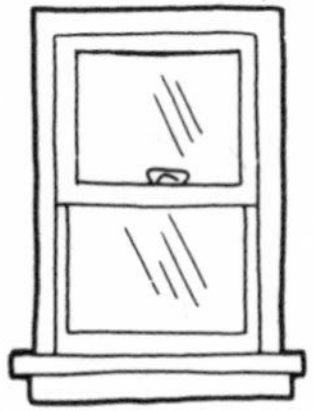

A6

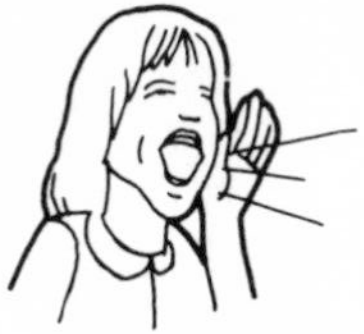

A6

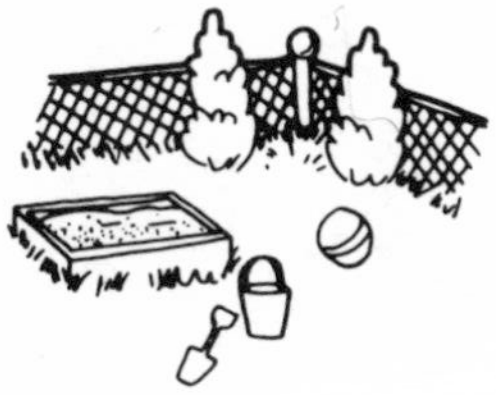

A6

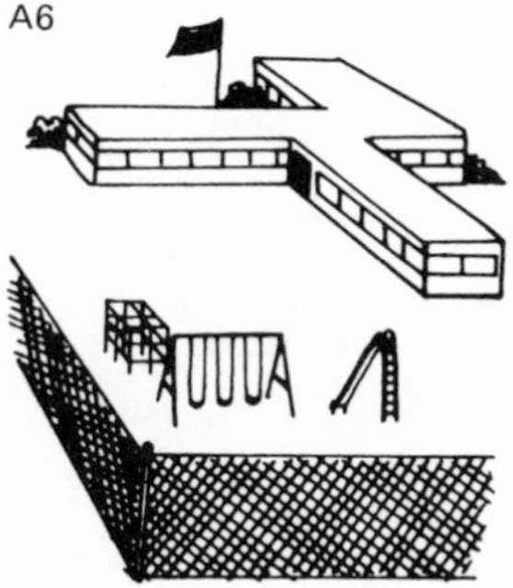

A6

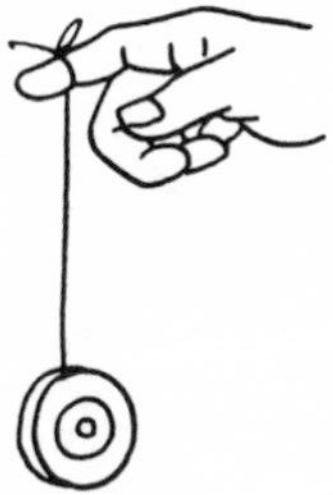

A6

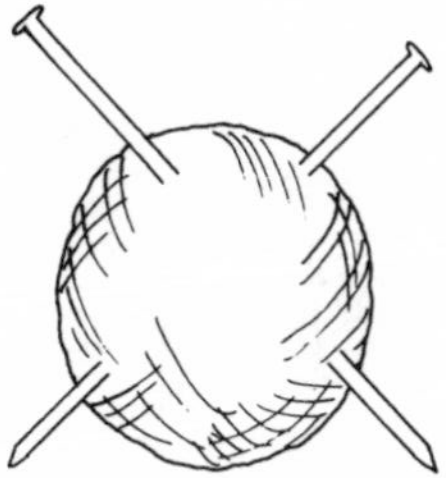

A7

A7

A7

A7

A7

A7

A7

A7

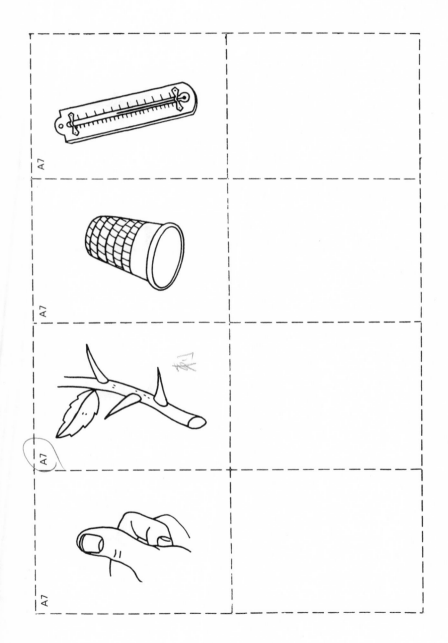

A7

A7

A7

A7

77

m m m m

f f f m

A1 f	A1 f	A1 l	A1 l
A1 l	A1 l	A1 l	A1 a

A1   A1   A1   A1

A2   A2   A2   A2

s

s

s

t

c

c

s

s

u u

u

n c

u

c c

n

p

r

p

p

h

p

h

p

r

r

r

r

g

g

g

g

o
o
o
g

d
d
o
o

e e e e

p p d e

U U U U

V V V V

A5 A5 A5 A5

A6 A6 A6 A6

N

W

N

W

Z

N

V

N

A6

A6

A6

A6

A6

A6

A6

A6

Y   W   W   W

Y   Y   Y   Y

sh

sh

sh

sh

ch

ch

ch

sh

A7

A7

A7

A7

A7

A7

qu

ch qu

ch u

ch u

th

qu qu

qu u

qu u

94

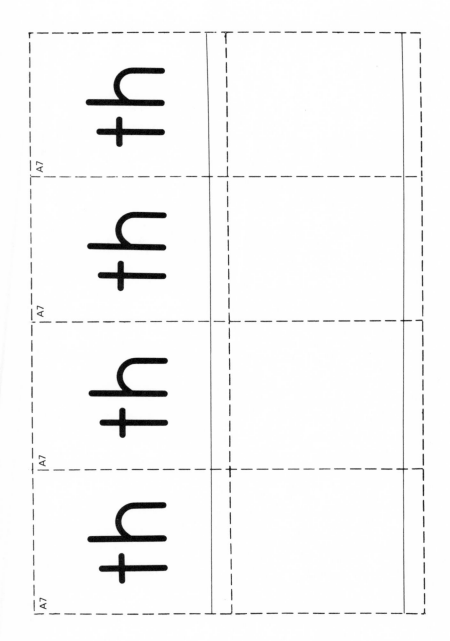

MATERIALS FOR THE READING GAMES

COMPONENTS OF READING GAMES

Each of the five sets includes the following components:

15 Word Dominoes—Main Parts
15 Word Dominoes—Endings
15 Word-Picture Cards
15 Picture Cards
15 Word Cards

ASSEMBLING THE COMPONENTS OF READINESS GAMES

The following pages contain all the materials necessary for assembling the component parts of the reading games. These pages are designed to be photocopied onto 8½″ × 11″ paper, two book pages per photocopy, leaving the back of each photocopied sheet blank. With photocopies of the component parts, it is very easy for you to make all the games. All you will need is glue, a package of blank 3″ × 5″ index cards, ten blank 5″ × 8″ index cards, ten business-size envelopes, and five 9″ × 6″ manila envelopes.

WORD DOMINOES

1. Photocopy pages 104–113 and cut the dominoes apart along the lines as indicated.

2. Paste the dominoes onto index cards. In some cases, particularly if you are working with several children at the same time, you may prefer to paste the word dominoes onto real dominoes, which are much easier for young children to handle. You will notice that there is an extra blank domino in each set. These can be used to replace lost or damaged dominoes or to make up your own dominoes when a child has mastered all the reading games.

3. Ten business envelopes, two envelopes for each set, will be used for storing the dominoes. In the upper-left corner of each envelope, write a set number, B1 through B5 (twice). Also write "Main-Part Dominoes" on one set of B1 through B5 envelopes and "Word-Ending Dominoes," on the second set of B1 through B5 envelopes.

WORD-PICTURE CARDS

1. Photocopy pp. 114–139, and cut cards apart along cut lines as indicated.

2. Mount cards onto index cards.

3. Stack cards into five decks according to set number and wrap them with a rubber band.

PICTURE CARDS

1. Photocopy pp. 140–149, and cut pictures apart along cut lines as indicated.

2. Mount pictures onto index cards.

3. Stack picture cards into five decks according to the set number and wrap each deck with a rubber band.

WORD CARDS

1. Photocopy pp. 150–159, and cut cards apart along cut lines as indicated.

2. Mount cards onto index cards.

3. Stack word cards into five decks according to the set number and wrap each deck with a rubber band.

After assembling word-picture, picture, and word cards make storage units according to the following instructions.

1. Label five 9″ × 6″ envelopes using the labels provided on pp. 99–103 (Set B1, B2, and so on).

2. After assembling the dominoes for each set, put both domino envelopes ("Main-Part Dominoes" and "Word-Ending Dominoes") into the corresponding large storage envelope for each set.

3. Next, assemble the word-picture cards for each of the five sets and place each deck in the corresponding storage envelope.

4. Assemble your picture cards and place each deck in its corresponding envelope.

5. Place your word cards in the appropriate envelopes.

LABELS FOR THE READING GAMES

The labels on pp. 99–103 may be photocopied and pasted onto 9″ × 6″ manila envelopes, which can be used to store the materials for each set. Note that the labels provide a summary of the contents of each set.

SET B1

Short-*a* words
Word Dominoes
    15 Main-Part Dominoes
    15 Word-Ending Dominoes
15 Picture Cards
15 Word Cards
15 Word-Picture Cards
Vocabulary
    man hat cat map jam
    pan fan can ham gas
    pad bat mat nap bag

Set B2

Short-*i* words

Word Dominoes

   15 Main-Part Dominoes

   15 Word-Ending Dominoes

15 Picture Cards

15 Word Cards

15 Word-Picture Cards

Vocabulary

   pin pig dig fix mix

   lid ship hit lip sip

   six fin sit kit bib

SET B3

Short-*o* Words

Word Dominoes

    15 Main-Part Dominoes

    15 Word-Ending Dominoes

15 Picture Cards

15 Word Cards

15 Word-Picture Cards

Vocabulary

    mop log rod dot top

    dog fox hog top hop

    pot box ox cot cob

SET B4

Short-*u* Words

Word Dominoes

    15 Main-Part Dominoes

    15 Word-Ending Dominoes

15 Picture Cards

15 Word Cards

15 Word-Picture Cards

Vocabulary

    mud bus tug jug sun

    cup tub bun run bug

    bud gum hut rug nut

SET B5

Short-*e* words
Word Dominoes
  15 Main-Part Dominoes
  15 Word-Ending Dominoes
15 Picture Cards
15 Word Cards
15 Word-Picture Cards
Vocabulary
  bed jet bell egg well
  pen wet men leg pet
  net peg web hen ten

WORD DOMINOES
B 1 Main-Part Dominoes

B1 **ba** ___	B1 **ca** ___	B1 **ca** ___	B1 **ba** ___
B1 **fa** ___	B1 **ga** ___	B1 **ha** ___	B1 **ha** ___
B1 **ja** ___	B1 **ma** ___	B1 **ma** ___	B1 **ma** ___
B1 **na** ___	B1 **pa** ___	B1 **pa** ___	B1 ___

SHORT-*a* WORDS
B1 Word-Ending Dominoes

B1	B1	B1	B1
t ___	t ___	n ___	s ___
B1 n ___	**B1** g ___	**B1** t ___	**B1** m ___
B1 m ___	**B1** t ___	**B1** n ___	**B1** p ___
B1 p ___	**B1** n ___	**B1** d ___	**B1** ___

WORD DOMINOES
B2 Main-Part Dominoes

B2	B2	B2	B2
bi	si	di	fi

B2	B2	B2	B2
fi	hi	ki	li

B2	B2	B2	B2
li	mi	pi	pi

B2	B2	B2	B2
si	shi	si	

SHORT-*i* WORDS
B2 Word-Ending Dominoes

b	B2 p	B2 g	B2 x
n	B2 t	B2 t	B2 p
d	B2 x	B2 n	B2 g
x	B2 p	B2 t	

WORD DOMINOES
B3 Main-Part Dominoes

B3 o ___	**B3** bo ___	**B3** co ___	**B3** do ___
B3 do ___	**B3** fo ___	**B3** ho ___	**B3** lo ___
B3 mo ___	**B3** po ___	**B3** ro ___	**B3** co ___
B3 to ___	**B3** ho ___	**B3** to ___	**B3**

SHORT-*O* WORDS
B3 Word-Ending Dominoes

	B3	B3	B3
x ___	x ___	t ___	g ___
B3	**B3**	**B3**	**B3**
t ___	x ___	p ___	g ___
B3	**B3**	**B3**	**B3**
p ___	t ___	d ___	b ___
B3	**B3**	**B3**	
p ___	g ___	p ___	

WORD DOMINOES
B4 Main-Part Dominoes

B4 **bu**	B4 **bu**	B4 **bu**	B4 **cu**
B4 **bu**	B4 **gu**	B4 **hu**	B4 **ju**
B4 **tu**	B4 **mu**	B4 **nu**	B4 **tu**
B4 **ru**	B4 **ru**	B4 **su**	B4

SHORT-*u* WORDS
B4 Word-Ending Dominoes

B4	B4	B4	B4
d __	g __	s __	p __
n __	m __	t __	g __
g __	d __	t __	g __
n __	n __	b __	__

WORD DOMINOES
B5 Main-Part Dominoes

B5 **be**	B5 **pe**	B5 **we**	B5 **e**
B5 **we**	B5 **he**	B5 **le**	B5 **me**
B5 **ne**	B5 **pe**	B5 **pe**	B5 **be**
B5 **je**	B5 **te**	B5 **we**	B5

SHORT-*e* WORDS
B5 Word-Ending Dominoes

B5 B5 B5

d | g | b | gg

B5 B5 B5

n | g | n | t

B5 B5 B5

n | t | ll | t

B5 B5 B5

n | t | ll

cat

hat

man

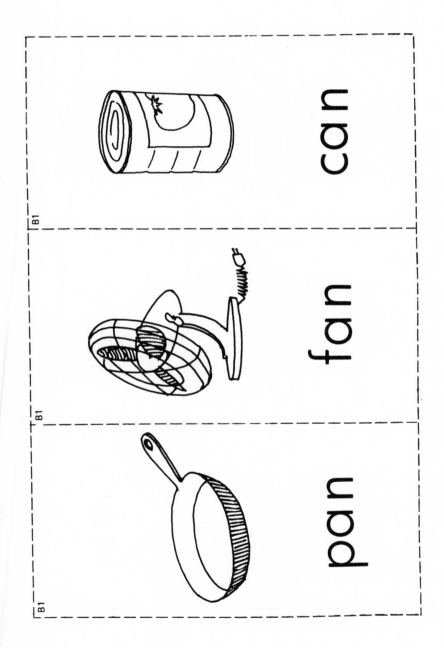

can

fan

pan

115

map

gas

ham

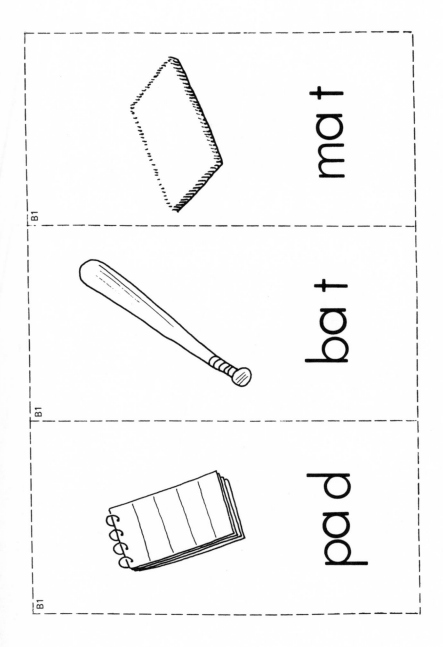

mat

bat

pad

117

jam

bag

nap

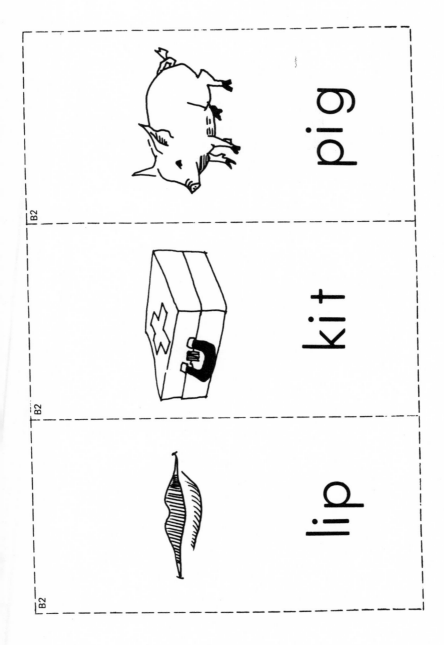

pig

kit

lip

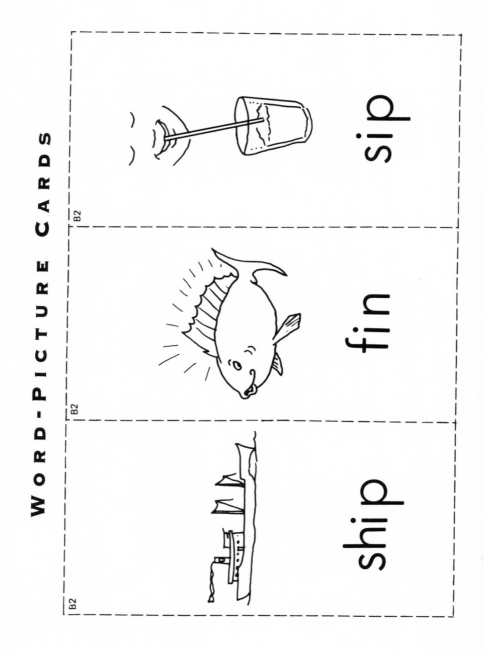

sip

fin

ship

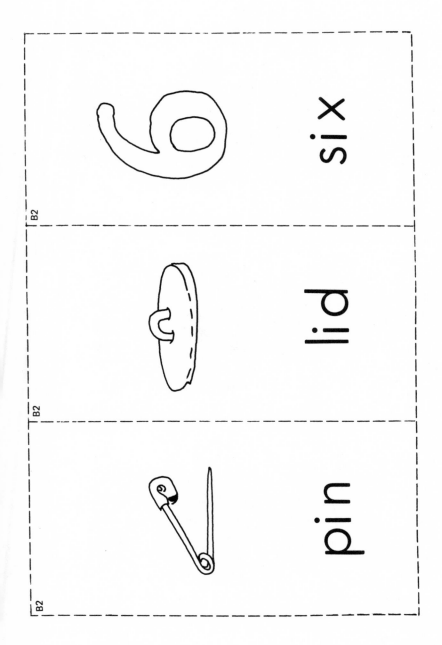

six

lid

pin

fix

mix

sit

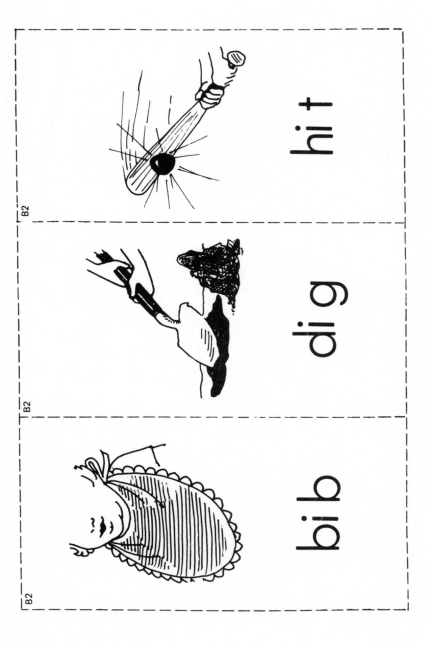

bib

dig

hit

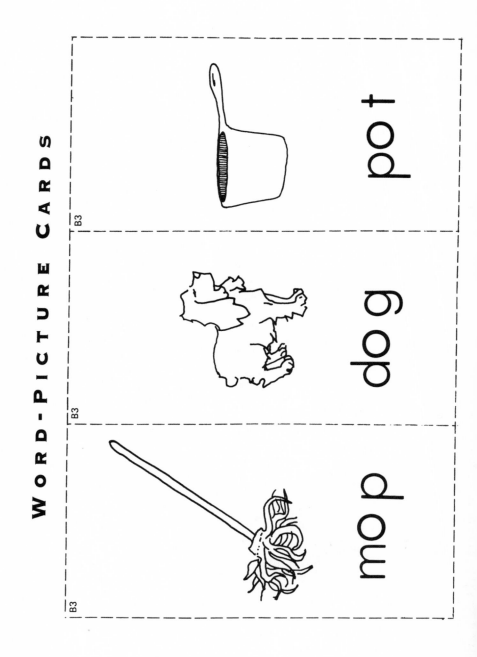

pot

dog

mop

B3

B3

B3

hop

box

fox

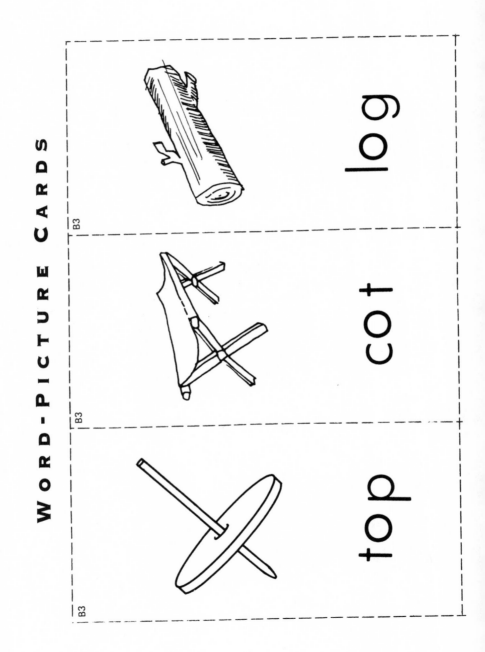

log

cot

top

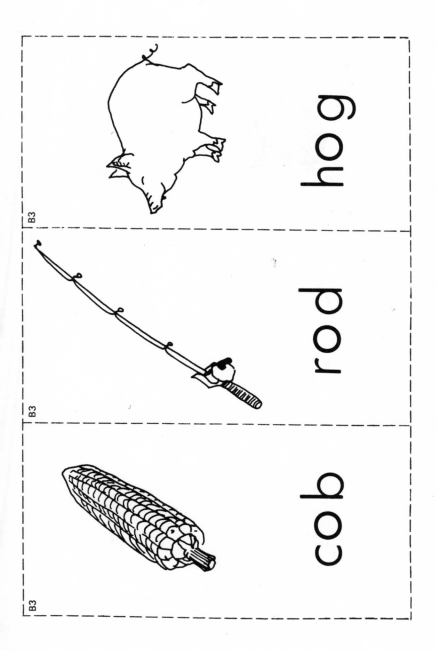

hog

rod

cob

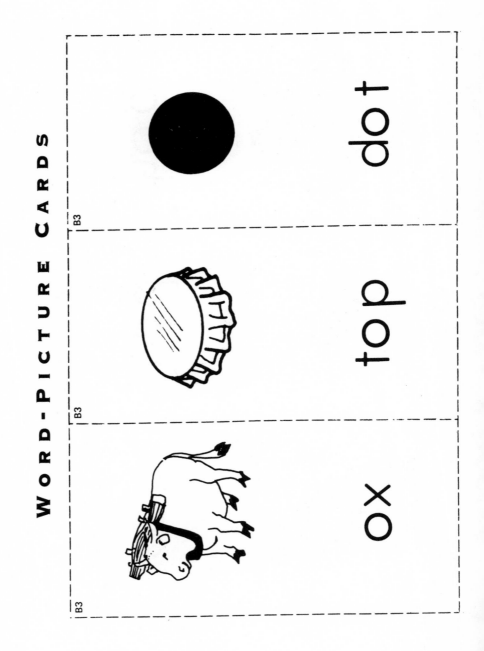

Word-Picture Cards

dot

top

ox

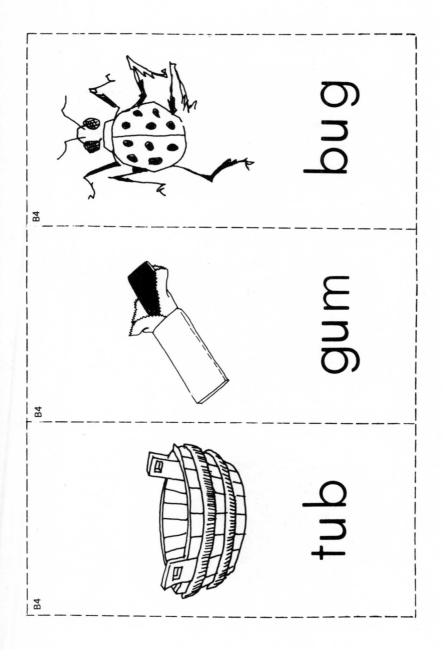

bug

gum

tub

bud

cup

mud

B4

B4

B4

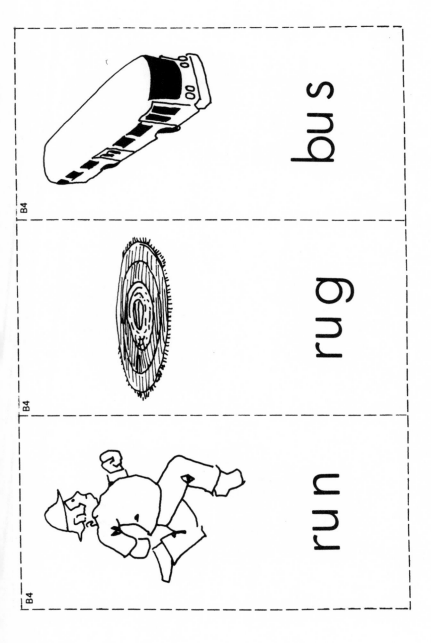

bus

rug

run

jug

sun

hut

B4

B4

B4

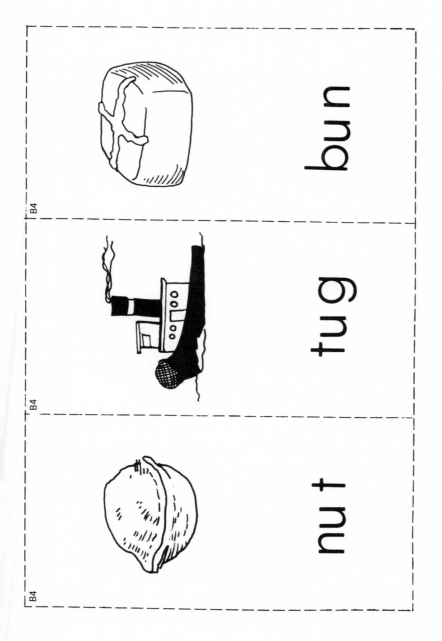

bun

tug

nut

Word-Picture Cards

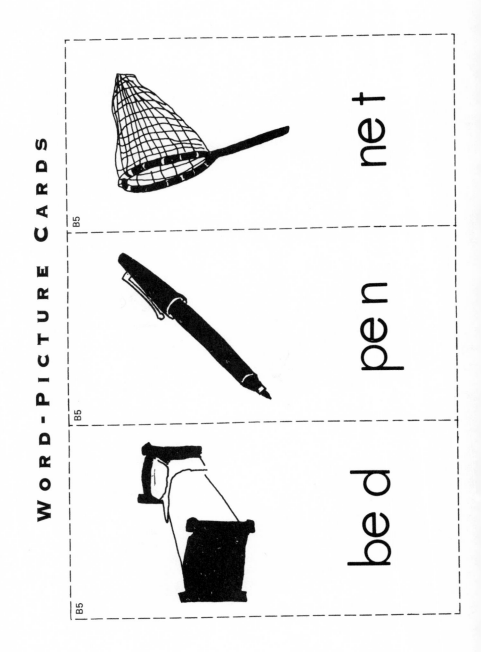

net

pen

bed

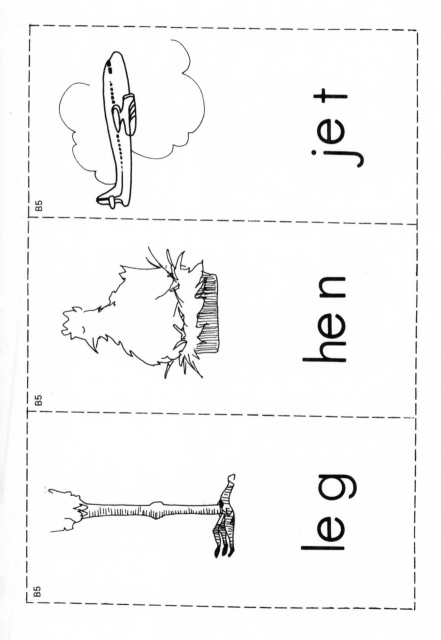

jet

hen

leg

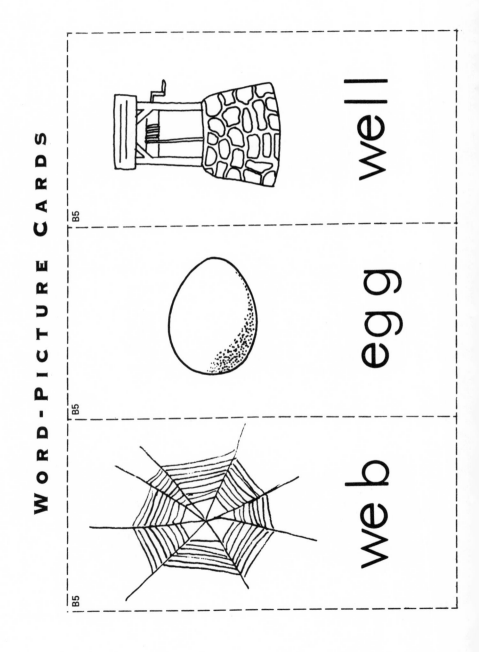

well

egg

web

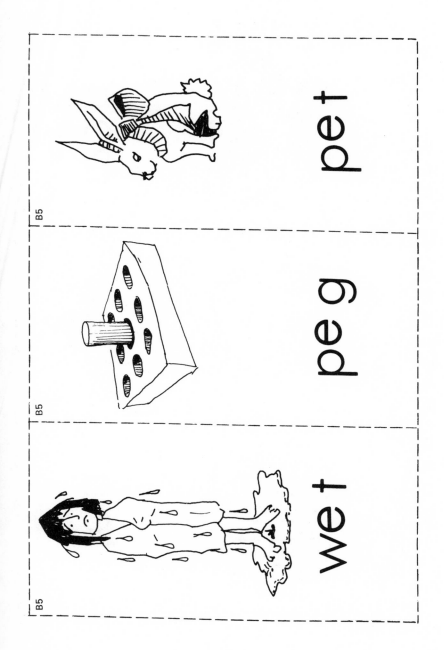

pet

peg

wet

B5

men

B5

bell

B5

ten

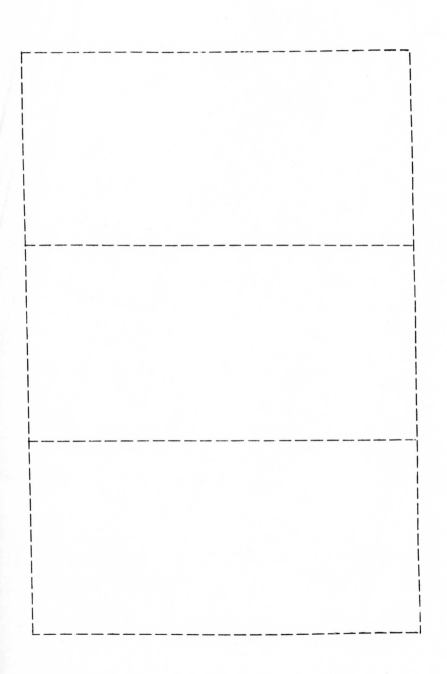

139

PICTURE CARDS

B1

B1

B1

B1

B1

B1

B1

B1

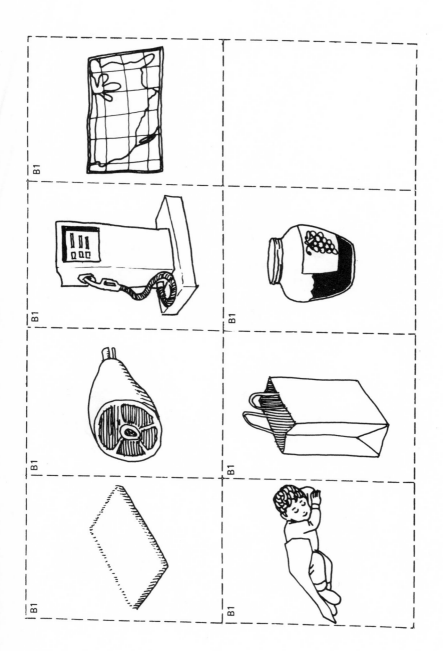

PICTURE CARDS

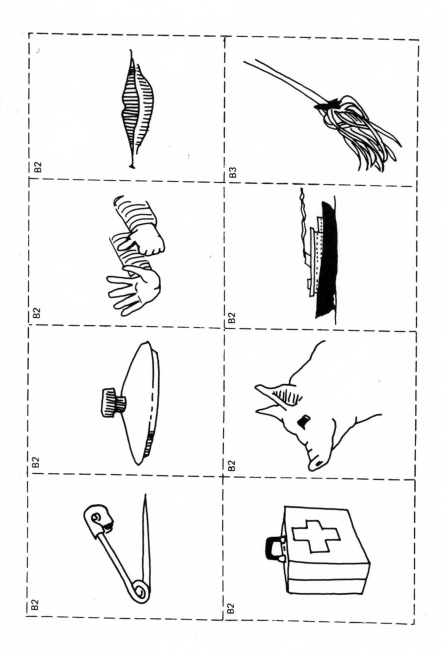

B3

B3

B3

B3

B3

B3

B3

B3

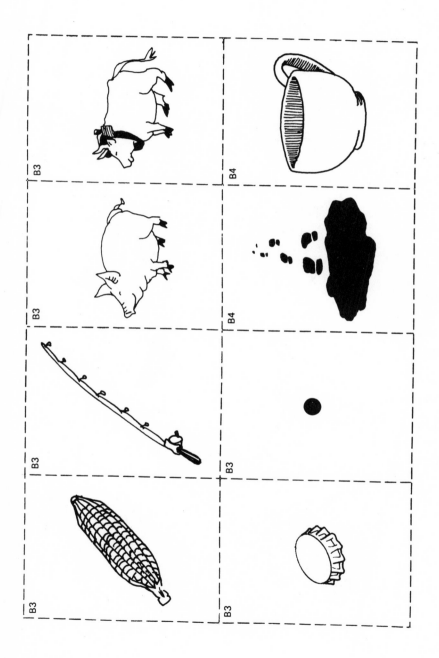

B3

B4

B3

B4

B3

B3

B3

B3

PICTURE CARDS

B4

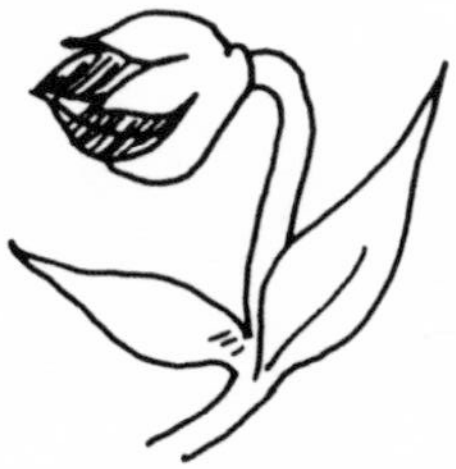

B4

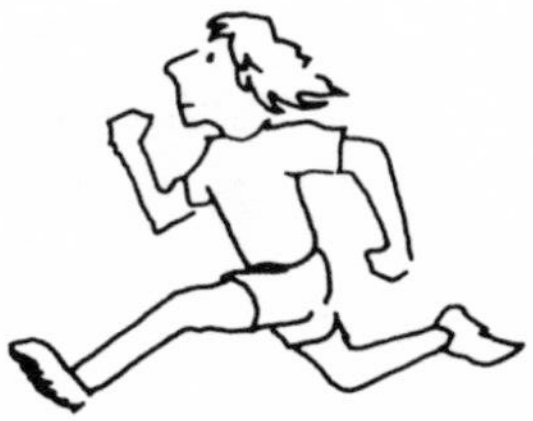

B4

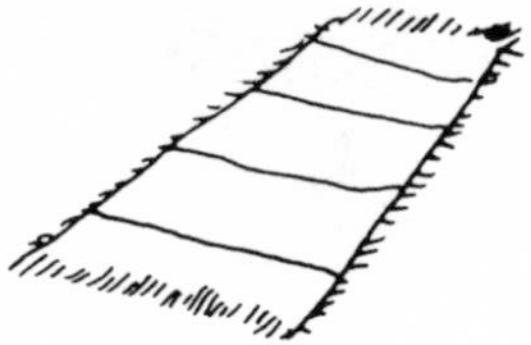

B4

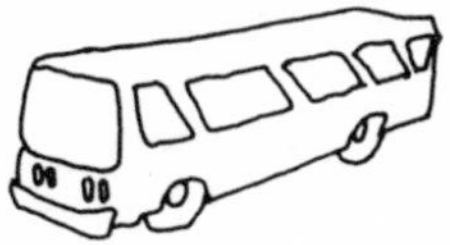

B4

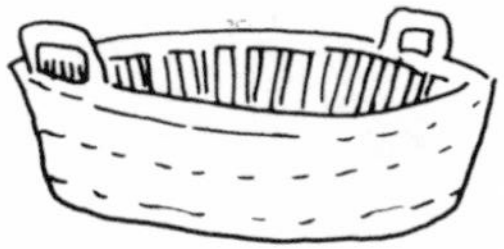

B4

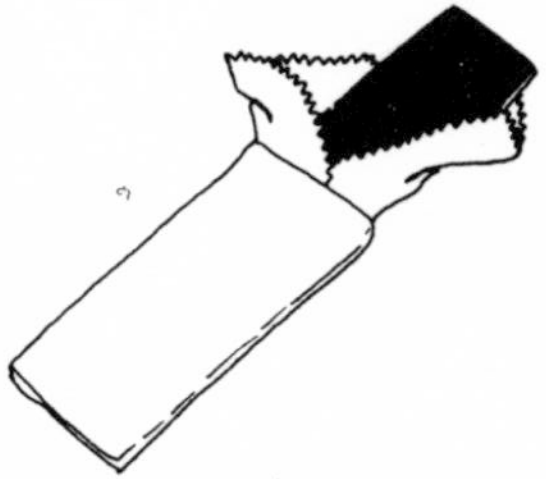

B4

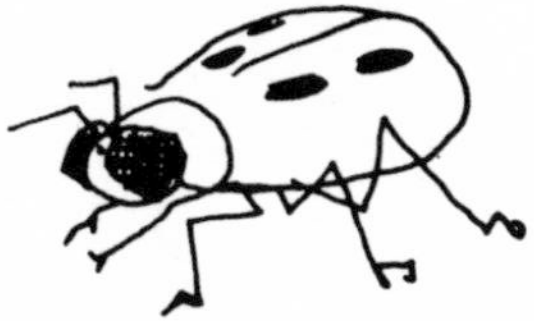

B4

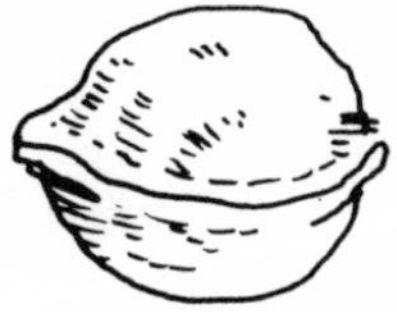

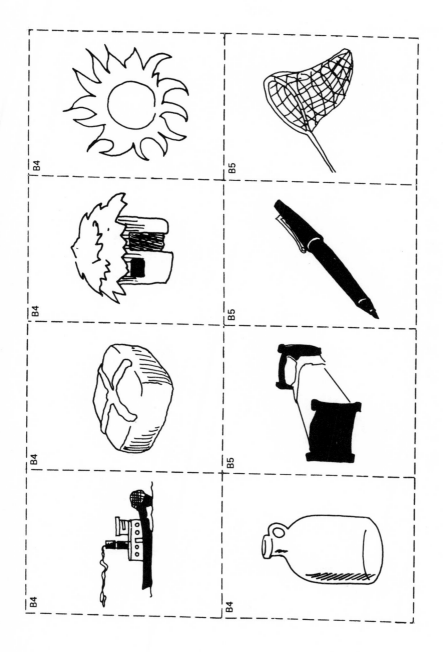

B5

B5

B5

B5

B5

B5

B5

B5

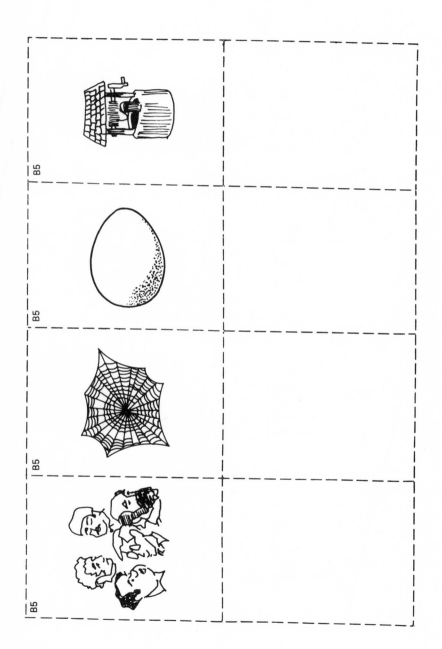

pan

cat

hat

man

bat

pad

can

fan

B1 B1 B1 B1 B1 B1 B1 B1

map

pin

gas

jam

ham

bag

mat

nap

kit

lip

six

lid

sip

fin

ship

pig

B2
B2
B2
B2
B2
B2
B2
B2

sit

hit

dig

bib

dog

mop

fix

mix

log

cot

top

pot

cob

hop

box

fox

B3 B3 B3 B3 B3 B3 B3 B3

top

ox

hog

rod

bud

cup

mud

dot

tub

bus

rug

run

tug

nut

bug

gum

jug	sun	hut	bun
B4	B4	B4	B4
leg	net	pen	bed
B5	B5	B5	B5

peg

wet

jet

hen

men

bell

ten

pet

B5

B5

B5

B5

B5

B5

B5

B5

web

egg

well

INDEX